COLONEL
JOHN A. BROSS

TWENTY-NINTH U. S. COLORED TROOPS,

WHO FELL IN LEADING

THE ASSAULT ON PETERSBURGH

JULY 30, 1864

COPYRIGHT 2015 BIG BYTE BOOKS

Get more great reading from BIG BYTE BOOKS

Contents

PUBLISHER'S NOTES 1
MEMORIAL 3
THE 20TH U. S. COLORED TROOPS 9
A MEMORIAL SERMON 38
PROCEEDINGS OF THE CHICAGO BAR 53

PUBLISHER'S NOTES

John Armstrong Bross is forgotten today, while Robert Gould Shaw, the commander portrayed by Matthew Broderick in the film, *Glory*, gained fame immediately upon his death that has endured. Both events are remarkably similar—two young Union colonels who lead African-American troops and who died very nearly one year apart.

Colonel Shaw, only 25 years old, from a prominent family and well-connected, was killed in the Second Battle of Fort Wagner, near Charleston, South Carolina, leading the 54th Massachusetts Infantry Regiment of African-Americans. He also wrote 200 letters during his service.

Colonel Bross is not even mentioned in most articles about the massacre at the crater before Petersburg in which he led his men of the 29th United States Colored Volunteers. As you'll read in his letters, he was very proud of his African-American troops and they loved him for treating them like men.

The assault at Petersburg that claimed the life of Colonel Bross and many of his men was a tragic mistake. The men were trained to make the assault after the explosion of the Petersburg Mine, a tunnel that had been dug, packed with 8,000 pounds of dynamite, and detonated to breach the Confederate lines.

General George Meade decided not to send in the colored troops, not because he felt they wouldn't do the job but because he felt if the assault failed, the blacks would be massacred by Confederates. This would have had political repercussions in the north. White troops who had not been trained for the operation rushed into the crater instead of around it. They could not get out and were slaughtered. Then the 29th USCV troops were sent but the delay had allowed the Confederates to move troops forward. The 29th was decimated. Ulysses S. Grant later said, "It was the saddest affair I have witnessed in the war."

Many of the events of Bross' life are given below. He was born in 1821 in Pennsylvania, practiced law in Chicago, and was married in

1856 to Isabelle "Belle" A. Mason. In 1860, just prior to the outbreak of the war that claimed his life, the 34-year-old listed a personal estate worth $500 (about $14,000 in 2014 dollars) and real estate worth $10,000 (about $286,000 in 2014 dollars). Living with Bross, his wife, and their daughter Cora in Chicago in 1860 were Belle's 17-year-old sister, Anna, and a 17-year-old servant, Dora Vanderbilt.

Little Cora died on July 8, 1861 and Bross wrote very poignant poetry in the field commemorating the loss, included below, about that event. The Brosses had two more children together. His expressions of love for his wife and children, and his willingness to die for what he believed mark him as a remarkable and, in the best sense of the word, sensitive individual.

In 1875, Belle married Azariah T. Galt, with whom she had one child. She died in 1900.

MEMORIAL

WHEN good men pass away from the world, it is often fitting, both for tribute and example, to commemorate their virtues, and to perpetuate the record of their lives. It is especially demanded, when so many men, turning resolutely from the tenderest relations of life, are giving themselves to their country, that such as have become conspicuous, by self-devotion and singleness of aim and effort, and to whom the service has been a literal laying down of life, shall be rescued from that dumb forgetfulness which so soon overtakes the dead. Their history and patriotic devotion should be held in lasting remembrance.

The subject of this brief memorial, is not alone in giving his life to his country; but his is high on the roll of heroic names, who, in this day of peril, have made a literal sacrifice of father and mother, wife and child, house and lands, yes, and of his own life; that the nation might live, and that posterity might enjoy freedom and safety. Such men must and will have appreciation and honor, as much wider than their own immediate circle of friends, as their virtues and sacrifices are known. For this do we write a record of his deeds.

John Armstrong Bross, son *of* Deacon Moses Bross, (now of Morris, Illinois,) was born February 21st, 1826, in the little town of Milford, Pike county, Pennsylvania he was the fifth son in a family of nine sons and three daughters. He received a thorough academical education under the pupilage of his elder brother, William, at Chester Academy, Orange county, New York. Entertaining plans for a collegiate course, he had fitted himself for that purpose; but circumstances prevented the prosecution of his designs.

Making choice of the profession of the law, he commenced the study of that science in Goshen, New York. Removing to Chicago, in December, 1848, he entered the office of Hon. Grant Goodrich, with whom he remained until the completion of his studies. During the Pierce administration, he served as assistant United States Marshal, and held the office of United States Commissioner, until the time of his death. He executed the duties of these Federal offices with conscientious fidelity and ability; acquitting himself in each case, to the entire satisfaction of all concerned in the discharge of the respective trusts. After concluding his duties as Assistant United States Marshal, he devoted himself to his profession, particularly to the admiralty practice, at once entering upon a successful career.

June 5th, 1856, he was married to Miss Belle A. Mason, daughter of Hon. Nelson Mason, of Sterling, Whitesides county, Illinois. Their eldest child, a daughter, lovely and precocious, in her short life of two and a half years, had become peculiarly dear to the heart of her father. The wife, and remaining child, a son of four years, survive to bear the loss of husband and father. The sweet, unconscious prattler, deprived of the counsels of a tender parent, inherits a rich legacy in that parent's bright example, and untarnished fame. Eight years of married life brought much of joy to one so happily constituted to render his home charming, both to himself and those who shared it. His nature was affectionate, his judgment cool and clear, and his temper disciplined and even. Endowed, as he was, with a keen relish for simple social pleasures, he was attached to his home in a remarkable degree. Therefore it was no ordinary sacrifice he made, when he left it in obedience to the demands of his country.

That this proved his greatest trial, is revealed in almost every letter written during his absence, his decision in respect to entering the army, was no enthusiastic impulse, but the action of his judgment as well; which is shown by the fact that he did not join the first volunteers, deeming his family ties too dear to be severed, while men with less to bind them' to their homes were offered in greater numbers than Government would accept. When, however, the progress of events made it necessary again to fill up the armies, the enthusiasm of multitudes had cooled, and exertion became necessary to secure recruits, he decided that duty called him to the field. Leaving the position he had attained in his profession, and the home so fondly dear, he devoted himself thenceforth to his country. During the summer of 1862, he raised two companies; one of which entered the 75th Illinois Volunteers. Of the other he was made Captain, and it became Company A, of the 88th Illinois. The feelings with which he entered the service, are alluded to in some of his letters, written from cam]), after having become accustomed to his new position. Under date of June 4th, 1863, to his wife, he says:

"You know I have decided opinions upon the duty that every able bodied young man owes his country; and often on the march, when I have been tired, wet and hungry, and no dry place to rest my weary limbs, I have been cheered by the thought that in doing, bearing and suffering all this, I was discharging that debt and duty. How glad I shall be when, in accordance with my own sense of honor, I may return to the dear domestic circle, the Mecca of my affections."

Soon after the battle of Murfreesboro, he writes:

"Officers and men arc continually dropping out from various reasons. Many, I doubt not, enter the army thoughtlessly, little dreaming what the actualities of war really are, and hardships soon cool their enthusiasm. I fully appreciate the kindness of dear friends who desire to see me safe from harm, but for *that* cause I have no heart to leave my position. I counted the cost at the beginning; I know its dangers, and possible sacrifice; I am one of those who thoroughly believe that blood must be shed to bring this controversy to a close. We are often heart-sick to witness the indifference of men and women at home, but it cheers me to feel how thoroughly *you* understand the motives which place me here. I do not know whether all can reconcile my position with the absorbing love of home which fills my soul. But it is that very love which urges me forward,—that our boy may enjoy ah the privileges of our noble, God-given republic. No other object could tempt me from a home so full of true enjoyment. You know I would willingly carry a musket, or be commanded by almost any one, if thereby I could do aught for my country. Yesterday, on being introduced to General Negley—'Ah,' said he, 'I saw you in *the Cedars.*' 'Yes, General, you did;' and the pressure of hands told more forcibly than could words, how our thoughts went back to that battle-field. The regiment has just been made happy by the receipt of packages from home. Though nothing is necessary to the vivid mental impression which will embody you in actual presence almost, yet there is something in the *tangible* evidence of love and remembrance from home. Reading the Psalms in course, brought the Thirty-Sixth and Thirty-Seventh for to-day, and I could not help feeling that with such friends, and such precious promises to sustain me, I ought to be content anywhere."

After a year's further experience, he alludes to the same theme; and gives evidence that his convictions of duty had not only led him into the contest, "but had been strong enough to enable him to endure the privations and exposures of the service. Writing from Virginia, June 5th, 1864, he says:

"The lighting has been desperate since the first of June; but we have been uniformly successful. It has been accomplished, however, at terrible cost of human life, and my heart has ached for the poor wounded soldiers. It is so different to come here and witness the *results* of a hard-fought battle. I have not felt the same enthusiastic tension of the mind, as on the field. Yet I also feel that in all history, there is no such example as is now shown by our people in their lavish expenditure for the care of the wounded. I am glad I have been here to witness it; and more than ever, am I proud that I am *one* of the grand army of the Union. I pray Heaven to grant me life and health to see the end of this war, that again I may enjoy the sweet influences of home in peaceful times: but whatever be my fate, I know I can give to my child *this one thing,*

His father fought for the Union and the old flag.

By taking command of his company, he had, like all volunteers, everything to learn. And probably the hardest task he found upon his hands at first, was that stern enforcement of discipline, which is the first necessity of military service. So different are the requirements of war from the conditions of peace, that no man can pass from the one to the other without feeling, at first, more or less of a shock to his sensibilities; and in a place of trust, he must be liable to many mistakes. But Colonel Bross entered upon the service, with the determination to discharge his duties faithfully. And he never, till the last, ceased his endeavors to perfect himself in his profession. By a study of the best models, he made steady progress in the art of command. It was probably to his thorough knowledge, combined with his strength of character, that he owed the perfect control he exercised over officers and men.

His regiment, the 88th Illinois, left Chicago, on the 4th of September, 1862, and went at once into active service, in Kentucky, first under Buell, and afterwards under Rosecrans. Its first battle was at Perrysville, Kentucky, but a short time after its entrance upon duty. The action is sometimes called that of Chaplin Hills. The regiment was under fire but a short time, yet it lost forty men. His conduct in this engagement, fixed him as a man of true courage; one upon whom reliance could be placed, in an emergency; and those who have had experience, know, that the first battle tries the man, and shows upon whom dependence may be placed in further scenes of danger.

Not long afterwards, General Buell was relieved of his command, and General Rosecrans appointed m his place. He entered upon his duties with great vigor, and pushed his enemy out of Kentucky into Tennessee. His first considerable engagement was that near Murfreesboro, at Stone River, where he met the enemy about the last of December. The main action was preceded by skirmishing of several days duration; but on the 31st of December, the right wing of Rosecrans' army was attacked at daybreak, and before noon, was forced back some four miles, and considerably crippled. The 88th regiment was posted near the left in the right wing, and held its ground firmly through the whole action; though it retreated under orders, that it might keep its position in the line. In the early part of the fight, it was attacked by an entire brigade, which it held in check and repulsed. It thus indicated the quality of its material, and the efficiency it had attained. Captain Bross acted his part in this battle, with perfect coolness, and his conduct was warmly approved by superior officers. The battle terminated only upon the second of January. On the first, there was but little fighting; the day being given to repairing losses, and the burial of the dead. On the second, the battle was upon the left wing, and the 88th regiment was not actively engaged. After this the enemy retreated. Captain Bross was on picket duty that night, and first brought word that the enemy were moving. On the next day the foe was gone.

A long campaign of peculiar hardships, was brought to a close by the battle of Chickamauga, which occurred, September 10th and

20th, 1863. Here again, the regiment saw hard fighting, and Captain Bross bore himself with conspicuous gallantry; extricating his company from a dangerous position on the front picket line, and as before, escaped all bodily harm, though death was abroad in all the air.

A beautiful instance of how God was "in all his thoughts," as well of his perfect composure in time of danger, is found in several dates of reading, written in his pocket edition of the Psalms, which he always carried with him; especially in these words upon the margin of the 91st Psalm, "Read at the battle of Chickamauga, during the heavy firing on our left, and before the action commenced in our front." Sincerely could he feel, "I will say of the Lord, He is my refuge and my fortress; my God; in Him will I trust."

THE 20TH U. S. COLORED TROOPS

When the policy of arming the blacks had been fully entered upon, and proved, by several trials, to be successful, it was resolved by the authorities, to recruit such a regiment in the State of Illinois. The endeavor was beset with many difficulties. Our State laws, passed by a so-called democratic Legislature, forbade the introduction and residence of that class of population in the State; and low politicians were ready enough to put the law in force, were there not also a strong public sentiment against it. The sentiment of humanity was so much stronger than the law, as to allow the blacks a being in the State; at least in most of the northern parts of it; yet the prejudice against them was never slow to exhibit itself whenever a favorable occasion presented. To undertake the recruiting of a colored regiment in Illinois, though favored and ordered by Governor Yates, was a work requiring no small amount of courage, patience, and self-sacrifice.

To find officers willing to accept such service, was easier than to find those suitable for the position. Men were not wanted whose object alone was promotion, or increased pay; nor indeed who were actuated by any merely selfish aim. It required the very best of capacity for command, and the most entire unselfishness of object Black soldiers, as a class, have more to learn than white troops. They need a patient, parental discipline, as well as strict military authority: and their efficiency, as soldiers, of necessity, depends more exclusively upon the capacity and humanity of their officers.

Looking alone to his earlier antecedents, Colonel Bross would not have been supposed likely to accept such a command. He was educated in the democratic faith, and held his political principles with the conscientious tenacity which characterized all his views. His mental tendencies were conservative; and he yielded but slowly to doctrines antagonistic to his long established convictions. He had been taught to regard everything which savored of what men were accustomed to call "abolitionism," with distrust; and it was only as the measures which contemplated a change in the status of the black population, underwent the deliberate scrutiny of his judgment, that he yielded to them. To become the commander of such a regiment, involved a change in his views and feelings, from those of his earlier years, than which nothing could more forcibly illustrate the *change* in the times. Yet for this service he was selected and detailed, and commenced recruiting in November, 1863. He established his headquarters at Quincy, in order to avail himself of the exodus of the black population passing from Missouri into Illinois, at that point.

Owing to the late day at which the raising of the regiment was undertaken, many of the colored men of Illinois had already left, to join the service in other States. The whole number of such, at that time, was known to be about seven hundred. Most of two companies in the celebrated 54th Massachusetts, had gone from Illinois, long before their own State offered them the privilege of enlistment.

Colonel Bross, as Captain of Company A, had gained a reputation for courage and energy, which promised rapid promotion in the 88th regiment; and also naturally pointed him out as the suitable officer for the new command. He entered upon the work of recruiting and drilling his men with all his accustomed industry. From the first, he decided that his treatment of his troops should be such as became them as *men;* and the result was, that he soon established himself fully in their confidence and affections. The undertaking in his hands was at once a success, so far as the proficiency of the troops in their ordinary duties was concerned. The filling up of the regiment, owing to causes alluded to, was not rapid. Having raised six companies, he was commissioned as Lieut. Colonel, April 7th, 1864. He was ordered to join the Ninth Army Corps, then moving from Annapolis to the field. He passed through Chicago, with his regiment, on the 27th of May, 1864. His troops were provided with refreshments at the "Soldiers' Best," and a number of friends presented the Colonel with a fine horse and equipments, as a token of their high appreciation of his steadfast devotion to the cause of liberty. The presentation address was made by Colonel K. A. Kastman, and was briefly replied to by the recipient of the gift. His response being entirely extempore, was not preserved, but a sentence or two is remembered by those who heard it. "When I lead these men into battle, we shall remember Fort

Pillow,* and shall not ask for quarter. I leave a home and friends as dear as can be found on earth; but if it is the will of Providence that I do not return, I ask no nobler epitaph, than that I fell for my country, at the head of this black and blue regiment."

From about 4:00 pm to dusk on April 12, 1864, surviving Union soldiers, mostly African-Americans, were massacred after a battle at Fort Pillow, having surrendered and thrown down their arms. The result was 350 killed and mortally wounded, 60 wounded, 164 captured and missing, 574 aggregate. The Confederates were led by Nathan Bedford Forrest and the rebel side insisted no surrender had taken place. A Confederate sergeant, in a letter written home shortly after the battle said that "the poor, deluded negroes would run up to our men, fall upon their knees, and with uplifted hand scream for mercy, but were ordered to their feet and then shot down.

The adieus were quickly said, and the troops were on their way; and Colonel Bross passed from the sight of his friends forever. It was the fear, if not the conviction, of many of them at that time, that he would never return. The perils of officers of his rank, in an active campaign, are always great; but in the service he had undertaken, they were felt to be largely increased. The cruel treatment of colored troops, and their officers, by the rebels, so far as their power went to reach them, was well known; and the massacre of Fort Pillow had recently occurred, to give intensity to the danger that adhered to this service. Of all this, no one was better aware than Colonel Bross himself. But his convictions of the rightfulness of arming the blacks, were clear; his faith in their efficiency, as soldiers, was entire; he had no doubt of his own duty, and he went forward to the sacrifice, without a murmur or regret.

His pastor tells us, that in a conversation with him, as he was about to leave for Virginia, on reminding him that his connection with colored troops would expose him to peculiar dangers, a tear came into his eye, while he said, firmly: *"If need be, I am willing to be offered."*

"There is nothing," as he was accustomed to say, "better expresses my idea of a soldier's duty, than Tennyson's description of the charge of the Light Brigade, especially the following stanza:

'Forward the Light Brigade!
No man was there dismayed,
Not though the soldiers knew
Some one had blundered—
Their's not to make reply;
Their's not to reason why;
Their's but to do and die;
Into the valley of death
Rode the six hundred."'

This he would repeat with such emphasis as often gave a pang to the hearts of loving friends, who remembered the dangers to which he would so soon be exposed, and now taken in connection with the manner in which he was sacrificed, seems almost prophetic. It clearly showed the direction of his thoughts, and what would be *his* course in similar circumstances.

The Ninth Army Corps had left Annapolis, before the 29th could arrive, and an order was received, directing them to proceed to Alexandria. General Casey was in command at Washington, and had issued an order for the regiment to report at his headquarters, near Long Bridge. For some reason, the order failed to reach Colonel Bross, and he marched directly past General Casey's office, through to Alexandria, and encamped, in ignorance of the General's directions. An order was thereupon sent to him direct, to report immediately at headquarters he was received with much sternness by General Casey. "Have you seen service before, sir." "I have, sir." "How came you to disobey *that,*" said General Casey, one of his staff at the same time presenting the order. "Are you accustomed to obey orders?" Said Colonel Bross, with emphasis, "General Casey, I obey orders with my life; your order never reached me." The mistake was, of course, discovered, and explanations were soon made. His air of resolute determination impressed the old General, and the Colonel was thereupon placed in command of the colored brigade, then at Camp Casey, near Washington. This position he held until after the battle of Spottsylvania, when, with his brigade, he was ordered forward to White House, where he remained till an opportunity offered to go to the front. At this time, the troops were rapidly attaining perfection in drill, and their discipline was every way satisfactory.

That his expectations concerning the rapid proficiency such troops might make, were realized, we may learn from his letters. One written when in command of the brigade occupying Camp Casey, Va., says:

"My men arc improving rapidly in all their duties. Captain Aiken is all I can desire in his conduct as commanding officer of the regiment. All the other officers seem to devote themselves to drill and discipline of their respective companies, while the men take pride in making all possible progress. It is with real pleasure I mount 'Dick' for battallion drill. The evolutions are performed with animation, and without noise and swearing, which certainly renders it much more agreeable to me."

Again, June 8th, near Old Church Tavern, he writes:

"My men keep up remarkably well; having become thoroughly conversant with the best method of 'getting on,' in taking care of themselves. So far from being injured by bad weather, their spirits seem to rise in proportion to the disagreeable state of the elements. Yesterday, we had a genuine alarm, caused by a dash of rebel cavalry upon our pickets in front. They captured a couple of dozen of our men, and killed one Captain. We were building breast-works at the time, and as soon as the alarm was given, the men I fell in, with great spirit. The musketry firing was quite brisk for a time, and we expected our cavalry to fall back on us, but it all became quiet without even a sight of the rebels. My men behaved admirably, and I was pleased that they showed no desire to slink or shirk, but came into line on the double quick. Our camp is in a dense growth of yellow pine, though we have an open field front. We had no breast-works as I said, yet the men took position as calmly as if in a fort. I went to the front of the regiment, where I could have a good *look*, and quietly walked along the lines to see that all was right. 'Colonel, we don't want you *out dar*,' broke through several stockades of ivory. After being in line about an hour, we stacked arms and returned to labor on the breast-works. My men handle the ax and spade in such manner as to gain many compliments on the neatness with which they finish their work."

General Grant had been fighting his way toward Richmond, and had succeeded in placing himself before Petersburgh, early in June. Thereupon an order was addressed to Colonel Bross, commanding the brigade, to detach one regiment to guard a wagon train to the front. His eagerness to be where work was to be done, led him to select his own, the 29th, and leave the command of the brigade, he reached the main army, and commenced work in the trenches, before Petersburgh, on the 19th of June: where he continued, to the fatal day which ended his life.

In the actual and exhausting labor of the campaign, he felt the necessity of filling up his regiment, so that it might be fully officered, and thus the better support his own endeavors. His wish had been to secure its maximum number from the free blacks, as he could thus obtain a more intelligent class of men than by accepting companies of contrabands from the Government, although these were proffered, and with his regiment at maximum, a Colonel's commission awaited him. As recruiting among the free blacks went on slowly, he had finally decided to accept the companies tendered by the Government, and being unwilling to spare his officers for recruiting, had applied for them. The order granting them, had been issued, and came just after his death.

Through the six weeks, in which the regiment was in the trenches, the weather was hot, and the work, of course, hard; but there was no complaint, and the service was cheerfully and faithfully rendered.

During the month of July, intimations were frequent, that some decisive demonstration on the part of our army was impending; and toward the end of the month, the information had been circulated, that' a mine was in preparation, which would secure to us important advantages. The army was therefore prepared for the explosion, but not for the disastrous results that followed. On Saturday morning, July 30, 1864, at forty minutes past four o'clock, the mine beneath the rebel fort was exploded; and at five o'clock and thirty minutes, a charge was made, and for a while, seemed to promise well. The line, for a short distance on each side of the mine, is said to have been brilliantly carried. The second line was gained and held for a time.

The colored division, under General Ferrero, including seven colored regiments, was then ordered forward. The fort had been seized, and the order to the black troops was, to take the interior line beyond. They had been ordered to take the caps from their muskets and rely on the bayonet. It soon became evident the work claimed to have been done by [General James H.] Ledlie's division,* was not thoroughly accomplished. The enemy's lines had not been sufficiently cleared, and such had been the delay, that the rebels had rallied in full force, and were prepared now to dispute, successfully, any further advance of our troops.

*Ledlie was reportedly drunk during the action and he was dismissed for his actions during the battle.

But they did advance, in face of a fire in front; and in addition, received an enfilading fire upon each flank, and also in the rear, from portions of the enemy's first line, which had not been taken. They advanced towards Cemetery Hill, which was the key to the entire rebel position. Cemetery Hill commands Petersburgh itself, and was, therefore, the objective point of the assault; and without attaining it, the attack, as a whole, must fail. It would seem, therefore, that such a careful disposition of the forces should have been made, as would render the attempt a *certain* success. On the contrary, the first assault was so executed, that no subsequent bravery could prevent a total failure; and *no* failure of the war, of the same dimensions, has been more disastrous. Hot that in a strictly military sense, the loss was so great, though it cost us four thousand of our bravest and best men: the military situation was the same after the attempt as before. In addition to the loss of life, the moral effect was intensely calamitous. It spread a gloom over all the land. It was widely felt, as a result, that we were making no progress in the war, and were likely to make none. All the friends of those who died in the undertaking, felt that their lives had been sacrificed to the most stupid and criminal blundering. If a soldier falls in a successful battle, his name is imperishably linked with whatever of lustre it sheds about it. History, poetry, and oratory dwell upon it But to fall in a failure, is to go down in comparative darkness, and history refuses to linger upon the theme.

It is not be settled here, as to whose was the blame of the failure in the assault of that 80th of July. But it is certain it was not that of the men who were there wantonly slaughtered, nor of the officers who fell with them. The criminality lies in a higher stratum, and is a question a court of inquiry alone can settle. Such a court was ordered, and commenced its labors—perhaps concluded them, but no result has ever transpired; and if it had, would most likely fail to give much more of certainty to the direction of public censure, than exists at present.

We are able to trace, by the aid of several witnesses, the individual course of Colonel Bross, from the incipiency of the undertaking, to his death. On the evening of the 29th of July—Friday, his regiment was lying in the rifle pits, about four miles to the left of Petersburg. About nine o'clock p M., the order came to march to the front of the fort to be exploded on the next morning. The order was at once obeyed, and by eleven o'clock, the regiment was in the position designated. It lay all night upon its arms, and at three o'clock in the morning, was roused for breakfast, and at four, formed in column. As this was the first desperate work undertaken by these troops, there was, perhaps, little of sleep on that night, for officers or men. One who saw Colonel Bross, at eleven o'clock, found him walking back and forth before his tent, seeming somewhat anxious and agitated; but he at once controlled himself, and joined cheerfully in conversation, talking over the coming struggle. Three of the officers had not yet received their commissions. As they could not thus claim the privileges of prisoners of war, they could be excused from going into battle if they chose. But from their love to the Colonel, they refused to avail themselves of the privilege. Singularly, they were the only officers in the regiment who escaped severe wounds, in the assault.

On the morning of the 30th, as the troops were drawn up in column, shortly after daylight, the mine was exploded, and the war of artillery began. Colonel Bross was at the head of his regiment, and Lieutenant Chapman states, that he saw and conversed a moment with him, and that he was perfectly calm. As the regiment was ordered to advance, it crossed our own rifle pits, and then the fort that was blown up. Here it was said that some three hundred of the enemy were buried alive.

The place was covered also with our own men, so that their bodies had to be passed over to get to the field beyond, over which the black brigade he led, was to charge on the second line. Here the men were cut down with canister, right and left. His officers saw their Colonel seize the colors, (five color bearers having previously fallen,) and rushing forward, heard him say, "Forward, my brave boys."

It is the testimony of Captain McCormick, that the regiment advanced in the beginning, through a narrow strip of timber, on reaching which, they received the first fire of the enemy. Our first line of earthworks was just beyond, and then an open plain, across which the troops charged to the demolished fort Here they received a severe cross and enfilading fire, in which Captain Flint was killed. The troops reached the ditch in front of the rebel lines, and distant about a hundred yards, where they were concealed a short time, and then charged across the space. Upon nearing this second line of works, they were met by an overwhelming force of the enemy, against which it was impossible for them to make headway. Colonel Bross had advanced to the parapet, and planted his colors upon it. But seeing how matters stood, gave the order to retreat, and just then he was struck by a minie bullet, in the left side of the head, and fell dead, uttering, as one says, in falling, the words, "o, Lord." The regiment lost one hundred and fifty, in killed, one hundred wounded, and from seventy to eighty prisoners. It went into the battle with four hundred and fifty men, of whom but one hundred and twenty-eight came out. Of the officers, Colonel Bross, and Captain Flint, were killed, and but one of the Captains escaped unhurt. Major Brown was wounded, Adjutant Downing was severely wounded and taken prisoner; Captain Aiken, mortally wounded, Captain Porter, slightly, Captains Daggett and Brockway, severely. There is a touching account of the manner in which the Colonel became possessed of the colors, given in the simple language of one of the Sergeants. "The} ⁻ were in the hands of Corporal Maxwell, who was wounded early in the advance. Corporal Stevens took them, but was cut down from the top of the works. Corporal Bailey seized them, and was instantly killed. Private Barret then seized them, and bore them to the top of the fort, but fell dead. Captain Brockway then took them, but was severely wounded, and let the flag fall. It was then taken by Colonel Bross, who planted it upon the parapet of the works, the furthest point reached by our troops. The Colonel then drew his sword, took his hat in his hand, and cried, *'Rally, my brave boys, rally!'* The men pressed up to him, but he quickly fell."

From the various accounts given, it is evident that the colored troops were required to do a work which it was impossible for *any troops* to accomplish; and that they did all that was possible, under the circumstances. The unanimous statement of those who saw the whole action, is, that there was a delay to charge upon the fort, after the mine was exploded; and that thus time was given for the rebel forces to recover from their first panic, and to man the surrounding works so as to be ready for the charge when it came. It is in testimony, also, that the first advance, made by General Ledlie's division of the Tenth Corps, instead of rushing forward at once, to gain the possession of Cemetery Hill, halted as soon as it came to the crater formed by the explosion. This delayed the supporting brigades, which when ordered up were thrown into confusion; and the gorge was soon packed with men, who became the prey of the enemy's batteries. The colored troops, under General Ferrero, were thus not ordered to the charge till nine o'clock, more than four hours after the explosion, when there was plainly no hope of saving the day. Yet without the least flinching, they rushed to the charge, and only retreated when ordered, and after most of their officers had fallen. Those who saw them go into the fight, have never charged them with any cowardice. It is their belief that Cemetery Hill would have been easily taken, had the previous charge been made in time, and with the anticipated success. For prisoners from the rebel regiments declared, they had been marched four miles that morning, and were there in time to take part in the thick of the fight; that at first, only a single row of men, five feet apart, stood to defend our attack.

It is affirmed, without contradiction, that among those who penetrated furthest, Colonel Bross was the very foremost man; and his dead body was found the most advanced of any who were left on the field.

The following letter from the officer commanding the division, does not require explanation, or admit of qualification:

"HEAD-QUARTERS, FOURTH DIVISION, NINTH ARMY CORPS, (*Camp near Petersburgh, Virginia, August 7, 1864.)*

Hon. Wm. Bross, Chicago:

DEAR SIR: Although not the first to communicate to you the sad intelligence of the death of your brother, Lieutenant Colonel John A. Bross, 29th U. S. colored troops, I can still offer you my sympathy in your affliction, and pay tribute to his memory. He was a thorough gentleman, a good soldier, and a brave officer. His loss is deeply felt in his regiment, and throughout this entire command. He was one of those of whom the service 'can afford to lose but few.'

His brigade commander, in his report of the action, speaks as follows: 'I desire to pay a tribute to Lieutenant Colonel Bross, 29th United States colored troops, who led the charge of this brigade he was the first man to leap over the works, and bearing his colors in his own hands, he fell never to rise again.'

Although he has left us, his example is still with us, to incite each and every one to do all, and to dare all, for the benefit of his country, and the suppression of this unholy rebellion.

I am, sir, very respectfully,

Your obedient servant,

EDWARD FERRERO, Brigadier General Commanding."

Falling where he did, and his men retreating, his body remained where he fell, and -could not be recovered. In the afternoon, the enemy established their pickets beyond where he lay, and buried him on the field. The ground at this time, is still within the enemy's lines; and whether his body will be recovered by his friends, is uncertain. But his is a soldier's grave; and no fitter spot could be selected than that where he- fell, in the service of his country, and in obedience to the will of his God.

Of his connection with the army of the Potomac, thus writes a friend: 'Though he had been here but a few weeks, he seems to have won the confidence and the esteem of the entire corps with which he was connected. All the officers speak of him in the highest possible terms. His regiment adored him. His conduct on the field was magnificent. As General White expressed it, 'all that can be acquired by dying the death of a Christian patriot, he brilliantly won.' His praise is in all the army. His record and his reward are on high. A Christian soldier could not wish a more noble death."

Thus ended the life of one who, as was expressed by his Major, "was everything that was good and brave." It is a consolation to his sorrowing friends, to know that he lingered not in suffering, nor was exposed to the cruelties of barbarous enemies, but "flashing his soul out with the guns," he was, one might almost say, translated to the world above; simply crying as he fell, "Oh! Lord," a prayer begun on earth, but finished above. In those last moments it must have been with proud satisfaction that he saw the bravery of his officers and men, and knew that *not one* faltered in his duty. Captain Flint died, while pressing forward, and the senior Captain, Hector H. Aiken, a superior and promising young officer, fell mortally wounded, and died, after enduring, with fortitude, untold suffering in reaching our lines.

It remains to speak of Colonel Bross more particularly in some points of his life and character, as yet unnoticed, and especially as a Christian gentleman.

His first special interest was awakened in his youth. He states, that when but eight or ten years of age, in accompanying his father to a prayer meeting, while passing through a piece of woods, his father knelt, and prayed with an earnestness which made an impression upon his mind that was never effaced.

Afterwards, and while at the academy of his brother, in studying Wayland's Elements of Moral Science, the truth as there laid down, as to man's moral obligations, fixed itself in his mind, and his sensibilities were much moved. Nor did the impression vanish. He deliberately made up his mind on the whole subject, and chose the fear of God; and though not at once making his determination known, he never afterwards wavered in his religious life. He united with the Presbyterian Church at Chester, Orange county, New York, in the year 1847. Upon coming to Chicago, he connected himself, first with the Second Presbyterian, and afterwards cast in his lot with the Third Presbyterian Church, with which he continued his membership until the time of his death. He was an exemplary and active member; being an attendant upon the church prayer meetings, and aiding in the Sabbath School. For many years he took charge of the choir, and led the service of song. He was, also for a time, the Superintendent of its Sabbath School, and until entering the army, took charge of the children's music. A strong proof of the affectionate estimation in which he was held by the children, was given, on his first departure, when they presented him a beautiful sword and equipments.

Nor did he restrict his labors to his official duties. At the same time that he had charge of the choir, and the care of the Sabbath School in the church, he was also a teacher in a remote Mission School, taking out a bevy of teachers upon Sabbath afternoons, during the entire summer of 1856, and thus maintaining a point of instruction in the region of what is now called the Williams Street School, connected with his church.

His religious character was one which entirely corresponded with his intellectual. There was nothing artificial about it. His mind was one that was singularly harmonious. Its characteristic was its fidelity to principles and friends. His aim was to *seem* to be what he *was*. While enforcing truth by example, he never made a display of religion, nor rendered it obtrusive. But his convictions were clear, and his will indomitable. All his conduct was entirely in accordance with the principles he held; and made its own appropriate impression.

His genial character made him a favorite with both officers and men: all feeling, that in him they had a sympathizing friend. One of them, returning after his death, stated, that, "on the Friday before he fell, he consulted with him upon home matters, which he would never have thought of mentioning to an ordinary superior officer." "I never knew," he remarked, "that the Colonel was a professor of religion, but any one observing his daily conduct, and calm, cheerful manner in the greatest danger, must feel that he was a Christian."

He felt his responsibility in the care of colored troops, and had thought and planned for their moral and religious wellbeing. He had thus commended himself to their confidence and affection, and was not only obeyed and respected, but loved by them.

One who came back with the Colonel's horse, remarked, "some said the Colonel was a religious man. He didn't know anything about *that;* but he was the best man he ever knew. He would not let any one about him say bad words, and he was so good to his men, that they would all be shot down before they would let him be taken prisoner."

In a letter, dated at Camp Casey, Virginia, May 18, 1864, there occurs this passage:

"I hope you will not think I wish, to make a parade of my religious profession, when I tell you I commenced my 'mess' in saying *grace;* and I shall continue to do so. I did not do this in the 88th. The 5th Massachusetts cavalry (colored), were here some days last week. The first afternoon they came, I entertained the officers at supper. They were hungry, and pretty well exhausted. As they took their seats, one young officer, in a half-serious and half-comic mood, asked me, 'if I would say grace.' I was standing at the head of the table at the time, having been engaged in seating them. I replied gravely, that it was always my habit at home, and should be pleased to do so here; and said it. There was a hushed set of officers for the time being, and very respectful conduct through that meal, though the conversation on military matters took a lively turn at the last.

"More and more, since I have been here, do I feel the weight of responsibility. The pleasure arising from the consciousness of *exacting* what is just and right towards men and God, has been great. I have felt the force of example, and shall try to continue it. If I have neglected religious duty heretofore, I will try hereafter, and not have the terrible words—'Ye knew your duty, but ye did it not,' addressed to me."

His remark concerning his table habits while connected with the 88th regiment, must not be construed to import a want of religious activity at that time, as all who were there associated with him state that he was always to be relied on in any Christian undertaking.

A young man, a member of his company at that time, writes to his mother: 'The example and advice of our Captain have led me to form new resolutions; and now, by help from on high, I intend to lead a new life." A more amusing instance of the force of example, was given in the conduct of his colored servant, who, at the first firing at Stone River, "made superhuman leaps to the rear." When remonstrated with, he protested he could not help it, though he declared, that in the future he would *never* retreat. After the campaign and battle of Chickamauga, wherein Bill had shown the strength of his resolution, the camp was exposed to shelling from Lookout Mountain, and many attempted to seek shelter from the enemy's bullets; Bill was coolly preparing dinner, and a colored man not far off was engaged in the same operation, when a shell burst uncomfortably near. With one huge bound, the latter threw himself into a ditch at the bottom of a ravine near by, when Bill cried out with scorn, "What you doin down dar? Why don't you sit *straight*, like *me* and de Captain?" Evidently thinking his own courage *now* quite superior to anything about him.

Of his professional character, and the high esteem in which the lawyers of Chicago held him, the resolutions of the Bar will eloquently speak. In person, Colonel Bross was about six feet in height, slender and compactly built His features were regular and finely moulded, and his countenance indicative of strongly marked character, and refined sensibilities. As an officer, his appearance was finer than that of a majority of those in command. A fine figure, a pleasant, commanding countenance, and strong musical voice, could not fail to aid him in his military duties.

Rarely do we find, combined in one individual, so many of those natural gifts, which rendered him a most genial and pleasant companion. His generous nature, delicate regard for the feelings of others, and unostentatious manners, caused him not only to be a favorite in a large family circle, but endeared him to all he entered into the enjoyment of those about him with a sympathy which caused even children to delight in his society. The strength of his social and domestic attachments was very marked. His friendships were sincere and true; his grasp of the hand, warm and cordial. He trusted others, and could himself be trusted.

Possessing a fine appreciation of the grand and the beautiful, his enthusiasm was always aroused by heroic action, or the sublimities of nature. The latter afforded him peculiar pleasure during his connection with the army of the Cumberland; the varied mountain scenery of Tennessee reminding him of places familiar in early life. Fatigue or weariness seldom prevented vivid transcriptions of their beauties, for the benefit of "loved ones at home."

Amid engagements of other kinds, he found time for culture in music and literature, having a passionate fondness for both. An indefatigable reader, with an uncommon memory, his knowledge was extensive, and his acquaintance with the poets, British and American, more than usually intimate. He was gifted with fine musical taste, and possessed a sweet voice, well cultivated. With the best productions of the masters of song, in this and former ages, he was familiar. For a favorite tune he sometimes arranged a few verses, as in the following song addressed to his wife, during a short absence:

The following productions, though impromptu, and of course only intended for the eye of most intimate friends, arc inserted, because they show both the strength of his domestic attachments, and the fervor with which he loved the cause in which he was engaged. This first, as he says, was "written hastily, while on picket," May 8th, 1863.

The father of Colonel Bross' wife was from Scotland, and her mother, a native of Vermont.

LINES WRITTEN MAY 8TH, 1863. SALEM. ON PICKET.

This day Mason attains the age of Cora when she died—two years, seven months, four days.

There is a boon to mortals given,
The choicest gift, bestowed by Heaven,
It blesseth, bringeth Heaven near,
'T is home, a wife, and children dear.
All these, 0 Lord, thou knowest are mine,
And for them all, Oh, Lord divine,
While mortals, yea, immortals live,
A husband's, father's thanks I give.
My children, twins in age on earth,
Thy father cannot speak thy worth
To him—nor all his heart-felt joy,
My daughter sweet, my darling boy.
My Cora, dear, thy precious form
Stands out before me mild and warm
With life, and sunny' smiling face,
And stamped with all thy mother's grace.
I see thee open the household gate,
While mama at the door doth wait,
And, tripping 'long the walk, I see
Thee come, and stretch thy hands to me,
To "kiss pa," quick with childish glee,
Delighting with infantile charms,
While close you nestle in my arms.
Ah! who shall tell the father's pride,
As with thee to the door I glide,
Receiving there a double share
Of joys that banish every care.
Oh! never, *never* can it be,
That from the grasp of memory
Those household joys can e'er depart;
They' re *anchored* safe within my heart.
There came a time (for angels roam
Around each dear domestic home,
When angels to their home above
Allured our sweet and precious dove
By fiat of the Infinite Love.
Oh, God I our hearts were crushed and bruised,
When that dear silver cord Thou loosed,

And yet from out our deepest grief,
Thou gently ministered relief.
And now, Tliou great Eternal One.
We pray as then—"Thy will be done,"—
While up from deepest grief we grope,
There comes angelic, star-eyed
Hope To soothe away our sharpest pain,
And *faith* that we shall meet again.
And oh, there is a thought to bless,
And raise from woe to happiness:
While that sweet form no longer here,
Shall e'er again her parents cheer,
She's safe from earthly tempests driven
O'er mortals here—she's safe in Heaven.
And as the glorious orb of day.
Sinks now behind the hills away,.
All nature calm and still and sweet,
The day and night in greeting meet,
Shall soon again in splendor rise,
Beam gladsome light in Eastern skies,
So shall our eyes with Heavenly vision
See that sweet form in fields elysian,
Arrayed in light—forevermore
She'll greet us on the Heavenly shore.'
And now I turn from that sweet gem
That sparkles in Christ's diadem,
And *Mason* in my heart I clasp,
With strong, convulsive, throbbing grasp.
A prayer I lisp—Oh God, most great,
Do spare his life—to man's estate
May he grow up—in virtue be
A model; and from vice e'er free.
My boy, a year has nearly gone,
And spring her gorgeous robes hath donned,
Since on thy lips I've kisses pressed,
Or locked thee in a fond caress.
Since when you first lisped, "papa"—"car,"
He's learned the dreadful trade of war.
And from the "picket" where his sword
Is ready for the rebel horde,
He sends you words you may not know

Until in years you older grow.
But mama, in her love for me,
Will gladly tell them o'er to thee—
Oh, then my boy, I charge you by
All things on earth and Heaven high,
By all privations, hunger, toil,
Papa endures on rebel soil,
By his heart-sickness—self-denial,
His leaving home—his *greatest* trial,
By every hope that has its birth
Of happiness in Heaven or earth,
Thy country love—stand by her cause,
Her Constitution and her laws;
And if thy father in this strife
With rebels yieldeth up his life,
A sacrifice upon the altar
Of freedom—Union—do not falter,
In boyhood, youth, at man's estate,
In cherishing a manly hate
Of all the giant sin and wrong,
Against which now a mighty throng
Of freemen gathered in their might,
Are fighting; and for God and right.
I pray that peace with gentle ray
May soon throughout the land bear sway,
And union, law, and liberty
Be ours—a blood-bought legacy.
But yet if this inhuman strife
Shall last until thy young heart's life
Shall grow to manhood—ever be
Among the brave hearts true and free,
Who give their lives for liberty—
So shall the debt thou owest to man
Be paid; with those who're in the van
Of progress, with their flag unfurled,
And giving freedom to the world.

The following was written in his tent, on the anniversary of his little daughter's death, having also just been made acquainted with the fact that *he* was to lead the *charge*, in which he so soon lost his life:

IN MEMORIAM.

Once more amid the circling years,
The day comes back suggesting tears
Of sorrow for the loved and lost!
Of brightest hopes of being, crossed
By one fell stroke; and in the dust
Those hopes in death's cold ruin crushed.
'T is well that memory fondly clings
Around her as she *was;* while springs
My fancy down the track of time,
And dwells in that ideal clime,
On what she *might have been;* a youth,
A maiden, full of love and truth;
A woman grown to please, to bless,
And graced with beauty, loveliness;
All these my fancy pictures now,
While in the West the sun doth bow,
And sink behind Virginia pines,
Illuming "rebel," "Union," lines.
So sank it o' er the prairie lea,
When that dear soul immortal, free
From earthly ill, to angels given,
Became a cherub safe in Heaven.
And since her father, in the strife
To save the nation's rights and life,
Has ta'en the sword, another thought
At times, within his mind has wrought.
If angels watch and guide the path
Of mortals in this life, and have
In battle or temptation's hour,
Death's darts to turn aside, the power,
Oh then amid the cannon's rattle,
And on the "perilous edge of battle,"
Is not *she* there to watch, and ward
Off danger, and her father guard?
And if in that all wise design,
That takes an insect's life, or mine,
Should rebel, hurling rebel dart
Transfix this poor and sinful heart,
Shall not this cruel, dreadful blow

Removing me from earth below,
From heaven on earth, all earthly joy,
My angel wife, my darling boy,
But introduce me to the being
Through a glass darkly now we're seeing?
Forgive, Oh Lord, our vain regret
And tears o' er Cora's loss; and yet
We're mortals; yet we'd love to live—
Enjoy all bliss this world can give—
Live, to enjoy sweet peace again,[5],
O'er all this land once more to reign—
Live, to enjoy a green old age,
Wife, children, Heaven's heritage.

Camp in the field, Norfolk R. R., near Petersburgh, Va., July 6, 1864.

Anniversary of Cora's death.

In his death, his family have lost more than any one can dare undertake to estimate. Society has lost a valuable member; the army, an accomplished and rising officer. But his country has gained a hero, and will keep his name forever. There will be a place for him in history; and though the enterprise in which he fell did not succeed, it was by no fault or short coming of his. Had all done their duty, as did Colonel Bross and his gallant officers and men, the undertaking had been a success as brilliant as any which the annals of war record.

All the consolation, therefore, which can remain from the pure memories of one "gone to the dear and deathless land," is left to the wife who weeps his departure, and is in store for his boy, who will learn his own loss only as years add to his powers of comprehension. The best of husbands and of fathers; honored and loved in society; useful and successful in his profession; trusted and confided in by the Church of God; an unselfish, earnest, devoted, heroic soldier; a firm, yet kind and manly officer; respected and beloved in all his relations, while in life, and dying in the very front of the battle, as brave men love to die—what more could be asked? While the land has such men and such memories, it has everything to hope and nothing to fear.

"His was a death whose rapture high,
Transcended all that life could yield;
His highest glory thus to die,
On the red battlefield;
And they may feel who love him most,
A pride so holy and so pure,—
Fate hath no power o'er those who boast
A treasure thus secure."

When there is even a shadow of uncertainty connected with the fate of a loved one, hope must still linger, suggesting the possibility of mistake, in the inevitable confusion necessarily following a battle. This agonizing suspense hung over the death of Colonel Bross; and not till the last of October, 1864, did conclusive evidence come in regard to his fate. Lieutenant Ridenour, of the 28th United States colored troops, a personal friend of the Colonel, who was severely wounded, and taken prisoner, was the first to communicate the sadly certain tidings. Lieutenant Ridenour was paroled October 7th, and being still too disabled to write, a brother penned for him, a letter, from which an extract is made, giving all that is now known of the Colonel's resting place:

"My brother was wounded in five places, and as he lay on the field the Colonel fell quite near him. He was shot in the left side of the head, and died *instantly* without a groan. My brother took from his pockets, his purse, diary, book containing letters, etc., hoping to save them for his friends, and supposing the ground would be held by our own troops. The result you know. Ho found himself in the hands of thieves as well as traitors, who deprived him of everything, even shoes, etc. As the men bore the Colonel off the field, my brother gave them his name, rank, and place of residence, entreating them to mark his grave; telling them his friends would spare neither pains nor money to secure his body. Brave and heroic, he died in a holy cause, manfully doing his duty, and his unselfish spirit went up from that gory battle-field, as we doubt not, to a haven of eternal bliss."

Laid to rest by rebel bands, the numerous tributes to his worth show that in many hearts he will ever have a place. Writes one who only knew him in camp:

"Though a stranger, I ask permission to assure you of sympathy in this great bereavement. His sad fate has been much upon my mind. The loss of such a one to wife and child, and that family of brothers, of whom he told me, is unspeakable, but the *gain* to himself I know is far greater. In all his command and intercourse, Colonel Bross was decided in his influence, and held the respect of all who knew him, as a Christian gentleman. He did not lose sight of the spiritual welfare of his men, while fitting them for their military duties, fiut aimed to make them soldiers of the cross as well as soldiers of the Union. Oh that more were like him."

A letter from one of the members of his company in the 88th, to a friend, exhibits the feeling with which he was still regarded by them:

"The men felt as though they had lost their best friend when they heard of the death of Colonel Bross. It seems as though the bravest and best are taken. It is a loss too, to our distracted country, when in her great peril she is not in condition to sacrifice, many such men as was he."

The following letter from a private, shows the devotion to him which was felt in the ranks:

"Camp near Petersburgh.

"Mrs. Colonel Bross:

Respected Madam: You will please excuse this letter, that I pen to you, but as I am one of the soldiers brought up under his discipline, I deem it my duty to address you. Allow me to say, that although a colored man, a private in the 29th, I found in Colonel Bross a friend, one in whom every member of the regiment placed the utmost confidence, for, and with whom, each one would help defend the country to the end. Yes, I can say with truth, they would willingly die by his side. I was with him from the time the regiment left Quincy, until he reached the land of liberty or death he loved his country, and fought for it, and may the Almighty never suffer his name to be blotted out of history. The 29th, with its leader gone, feels there is no such commander under the sun, to lead it forward and cheer it up. He was loved by everyone, because he was a friend to every one. God has received him unto himself, and may he give peace to the hearts of us who loved him. Weep not for him who was one of God's chosen ones, who tried to deliver his people out of Egypt. But his appointed time had come to be changed, and God works all things for the best. Fearing I might tire your patience with my poor letter, I will close.

Respectfully,

WILLIS A. BOGART."

A few extracts are appended from letters written by the officers of his regiment, all breathing the love and confidence with which he ever inspired his associates. Such testimonials are numerous, but a few will suffice:

"HEAD-QUARTERS 29th U. S. COLORED TROOPS.

MRS. BROSS:

My Dear Friend: I can assure you we all participate in your heavy affliction. The Colonel was endeared to us all. His virtues, his noble, open, and frank heart, attracted all, and compelled admiration. Always sincere in his motives, his greatest care was to act honestly and justly. He was not only brave on the field, but possessed that moral courage which sustained him in the camp. Throughout the whole Division he was known and loved, and the universal expression is, "had he only lived." Cheerful and pleasant under the most trying circumstances, he was ever ready for duty without a murmur.

How he enjoyed singing. At times when everything seemed dull and stupid, his clear voice would lead some well-known tune, in which he would have us all join. Soon stupidity would be changed to pleasure; and all gradually partaking of his spirit, would be merry and happy. I will not strive to offer comfort; religion only can soften such calamities.

Whenever I recall the scenes of that dreadful day, feelings of sorrow and regret inevitably arise. Before day we were up and ready. Every one felt the danger awaiting him, and there was unusual silence. All seemed occupied with their own thoughts. The Colonel came up to me, and we had a few moments of cheerful conversation. Soon the artillery opened—the musketry was distinctly heard—the conflict had commenced. In perfect silence we moved forward. My last interview with the Colonel was while wo were halted in the covered way. Captain Aiken and Lieutenant Gale were also there. Few words were exchanged, our thoughts, as usual at suth times, straying homewards. We little knew then that by incapacity and wanton neglect, thousands of lives were to be sacrificed. Again we were moving forward. The outer line of works was passed, and wo were hastening up the hill to the fort. Here, friend and foe, living and dying, were heaped together, causing us to halt in the midst of a destructive fire of both musketry and artillery. I well remember 3 how he looked, standing in the midst, his countenance lighted up with steadfast hope and an almost superhuman courage, he cried out, "Forward, 29th," and we moved on over the mass. The men were falling thick and fast, and soon my turn came. Lying on the field, I felt the auspicious moment had passed. His form was ever a prominent mark. Turning to Captain Brockway, he said, [11] bring forward the colors." Then seizing them in his own hand he cried, "Follow me, my men." But it was in vain; the enemy were concentrated. It was madness for us to charge where three Divisions had already failed. As we were ordered back, the Colonel was seen endeavoring to rescue the colors. Standing upon the parapet he said, "The man who saves those colors shall be promoted." The fatal ball came, and he fell, but the legacy of his bright example and the memory of his noble deeds remain. The intense sorrow and grief of that night I will not attempt to portray.

.

With deepest sympathy,

FRED. A. CHAPMAN, Lieutenant 29th V. S. Colored Troops."

IN FRONT OF PETERSBURG.

"MRS. COLONEL JOHN A. BROSS:

Dear Madam: With deepest sorrow I attempt to tell you something of the • relations our regiment sustained to our lamented Colonel, though I know I shall fail to express my veneration for that noble, generous soul, who has so heroically given himself a sacrifice for the liberties of our country. His spirit has gone, but his noble acts and example are left, to his child, and to us, well worthy our emulation. May his boy as he grows to manhood, show himself worthy such a father. We too shall be wise if we follow in his footsteps of usefulness, and labor as did he, all forgetful of self, for the good of others. Your husband, loved and lamented by all who knew him, with every thought and impulse so pure, richly bore that beautiful and significant name, "a Christian soldier." I have seen him under circumstances that tried men's souls, and know how steadfastly he maintained his Christian consistency and the integrity of his character.

The officers and men of the regiment, which, through his unceasing efforts, became what it was, offer you their fullest sympathy. We know your loss is great; but we too miss him, and you hardly know how sadly. I had learned to love him as a brother, and in memory of him, tears *will* come. All who knew him, were forced to respect his superior character. I sometimes feel as if he had a presentiment that he would not survive the charge. On the evening of July 6th, in conversation concerning the anticipated enterprise, though he said comparatively little of himself, yet his few words were full of meaning. Ho said the undertaking would be dangerous, and many must fall; he might be among the number; but let the danger be what it might, he should go at the head of the regiment wherever it was ordered. Two men of Company D, saw him fall, and made efforts to carry him away, but could not and save themselves. I know there is not a man in the regiment who would not have saved him at any cost, had it been possible, for he was idolized by them all.

To us, it seems as if one whose life was so useful, should have been spared; but we must trust him in the hands of our Heavenly Father who doeth all things well. That we may all meet him there, is the prayer of his devoted friend,

J. J. GOSPAR,

Lieutenant and Q. M. 29th Colored Troops." "Near Petersburgh, Oct. 20th, 1864.

"Mrs. Colonel Bross:

Dear Madam: I should have written you before concerning the sad events of July 30th, and the deep loss we there sustained, had I not been among the wounded myself, and but recently able to return to the regiment. Our Colonel was a man universally beloved by officers and men. His life among us was so free from any fault, so consistent as a Christian, that it challenged and won our entire confidence and love. In the management of his men, he was firm, yet kind, and though, as becomes an officer, a rigid disciplinarian, he happily had the judgment to blend kindness with discipline, and justice with moderation. His associations with his officers were of so generous a nature, that they seemed more of friend than commander. While he had their utmost respect, they felt that in him they had a friend ever ready to sympathize in their troubles. Though showing no partiality, we yet knew he noted the different abilities of those in his command. His name is often heard among the men, who think, and truly, that they will never again be led by a man in whom they can have such perfect confidence as they had in Colonel Bross. His death shows us his true bravery, almost rashness. Being myself wounded early in the engagement, I did not see him fall, but I knew the fatal ball came while he was at the head of the regiment, nobly battling for the right. While we must ever mourn his loss, we must still glory in his sacrifice for such a holy cause; and we believe his name will be handed down to future generations as one who fell in sustaining the liberties of our country. He died as became a brave, true-hearted, Christian soldier. His whole regiment deeply feel his loss; and we who survive, hoping to lead *his* men to other fields of battle, deeply sympathize with his friends and family. For if our loss is so great, how overwhelming must it be to them?

With much respect, yours, etc.,

THOS. A. CONANT,

First Lieutenant 20th U. S. Colored Troops.'-

Where there are so many officers and friends who write so kindly of him, it seems difficult to make suitable selections.

"HEAD-QUARTERS 29TH U. S. COLORED TROOPS.

Before Petersburgh, September 5th, 1864.

"HON. WM. BROSS:

Bear Sir: I would esteem it a great kindness if you would send me a card Photograph of my late much lamented find highly esteemed Colonel.

We had many happy times together during our—to me, alas! too short—acquaintance. When he visited me at the hospital, we used to make these old Virginia woods ring with auld Scotch songs. "My Nannie's awa," was a special favorite of his. He was delighted to hear me recite or read Burns, and many a hearty laugh we had at our "Immortal Bobby," and my Scotch pronunciation. Or we would start some sacred tune: "Sweet Hour of Prayer,"

"Marching Along," "A Light in the Window for Thee, Brother," etc. The two former he taught me.

I well remember the night we crossed the James. We had a long hot day's march on foot; his horse was sick. We were resting on an old stump when we received orders directing me to report to the hospital. He said, I 'Doctor, I am glad you are going to the hospital; if anything should happen to me or my boys, we shall get the best attention, and if I am wounded, I wish yon to attend to my case; I will not have any of these drinking Surgeons touch me." Then turning to an Orderly, he said, "call the officers." When they were around him, he said, "Now, gentlemen, we are expecting to storm those works to-night or to-morrow morning early, and I wish it thoroughly understand that *not a man is to leave his post to assist the wounded—no matter who falls, /, or anybody else. Let the wounded lie where they fall, and* PRESS ON." We then lay down on that corn-field—little thought I it was the last night we should spend together.

This war, and that of the Crimea, have deprived me of many warm friends, but this last is the severest trial of all. Be assured I should prize one of his pictures very highly.

I am sir, very respectfully,

Your obedient servant,

D. MACKAY,

Surgeon 29th U. S. Colored Troops."

The following lines in memory of Colonel Bross, are from the pen of a stranger, who, as she says, "gained her knowledge of his political and religious principles, and of his life and death, from the columns of the newspapers. Who would not admire, nay, reverence such a patriotic, self-denying spirit? Who could hesitate to pay tribute, humble though it be, to the memory of a *martyr* in the cause of freedom? Dear and sacred forever be the spot where he rests!"

A MEMORIAL SERMON

IN HONOR OF THE

LIFE AND SERVICES

LIEUT. COL. JOHN A. BROSS,

WHO FELL WHILE LEADING HIS TROOPS IN

THE ASSAULT AT PETERSBURG

JULY 30, 1864.

PREACHED IN THE THIRD PRESBYTERIAN CHURCH, CHICAGO, DECEMBER 11TH, 1864,

BY

ARTHUR SWAZEY, PASTOR.

SERMON

MATTHEW 10: 34.—"Think not that I am come to send peace on earth: I came not to send peace, but a sword.

The ways of wisdom are ways of pleasantness, and all her paths are peace. Wisdom is love promising better things, crying at the gates: "Riches and honor are with me, yea, durable riches and righteousness. My fruit is better than gold, and my revenue than choice silver. I cause those that love me to inherit substance; and I will fill their treasure." The Prince of Peace, by whom "grace and truth" came into the world, calls after men with the offer of rest, and foretells a time when he will have made a new heaven, and a new earth, and there shall be no more death, neither sorrow nor crying, neither shall there be any more pain.

Had we no further instruction, and no experience in the methods by which goodness and truth work order into individual life, and into history, it would be quite natural for us to conclude upon turmoil as a sign of the absence of progress in knowledge and piety, and to expect the easy and graceful triumph of true righteousness. And indeed, with all our sources of knowledge, there are not wanting those who insist, that all courses which provoke the passions of men, are, by that sign, contrary to the peaceableness of true wisdom, and who see, in the sharp conflict of opinion, and the convulsions of society, only the reign of blind and malignant forces, by which the world is turned upside down. But whatever theories we entertain as to the methods by which wisdom ought to acquire her dominion, the fact glares out upon us, that false opinions, and corrupt interests, never surrender without a struggle, that wisdom often requires of her children gifts and sacrifices, and that the kingdom of God is extended by ceaseless conflict.

The Prince of Peace gives peace to all men who trust in him, and obey his counsels. He has promised, and is preparing a universal peace; but he warns his disciples that stripes, imprisonment, and death are in store for those who hail the day of promise, as well as judgments for those who resist its coming. "Think not that I am come to send peace on the earth. I came not to send *peace*, but a SWORD."

This declaration of the Lord contains in it no warrant for violence. It furnishes no apology for the spirit of vengeance. It proposes to gain no advantage by force of arms. Upon the question of the justifiableness of war, it has no direct bearing. It is a simple assertion, that the utterance, and maintenance of the truth, will insure turmoil and confusion, inflame the passions of men, give rise to hatreds, divide families, array man against man, and provoke the shedding of blood. His own appearing in the world, instead of being hailed with gladness, excited the wrath of those to whom he offered the words of life, to such a degree, that they not only maligned him as a creator of sedition, but nailed him as a felon to the tree. To confess his name was to earn the contempt of society, the inheritance of an outcast, and a martyr's doom. To make a convert to his doctrine was, so far, to undermine the order of things to which the many clung as to their very lives, and therefore to provoke the vengeance of all orders of men. The truth would commend itself to some who would glory in confessing his name, and so become propagandists of the gospel. Thence divided families, and bitter feuds, and bloody wars, till the triumph.

It is not necessary to think very profoundly, in order to discover some of the reasons why right opinions provoke serious conflict.

The first thing we observe is the *self-asserting quality* of truth. It is no *vis enertice*. It is a vital something, demonstrative, endowed with powers; a tremendous cause, effecting always a result. A burning candle is not merely a wick ignited; it gives light. An acorn is not merely a solid inch of matter; it is a mighty tree getting birth. The lightning is no mere pyrotechnic blaze; it is the bolt of God. Truth is no mere phenomenon,—no mere plaything; it is the light, the seed-power, the sword of God.

Truth has *a presence* which can no more be hid or ignored, than a great sold appearing among men. It would be as natural to think of Moses, or Peter the Great living in the world unrecognized, as to think of truth not commanding the attention of men.

The self-asserting quality of truth is necessitated by the strong convictions, and sense of its worth in those that possess it. To them it is the pearl of great price, the solvent of many hard problems. It mends misfortunes, opens many reservoirs of happiness, is an alterative for misery, the harbinger of a better day. It is itself excellence, the true good. The end of life is to acknowledge and obey it.

And, further, truth compels believers to publish it. It is joy-giving. Like the woman who found 'the lost piece of silver, they must call together their neighbors and rejoice over it. Fire is shut up in their bones; they must speak. She scorns them when they are silent, scourges them as cowards when they do not partake of her boldness, and honors them with a sense of manhood and personal worth when they publish her decrees.

You might as well bid grandeur and beauty put off the investiture of God, the sea not to shimmer in the sun, flowers and plants to be inodorous, winds not to blow, hatred not to hate, love not to love, as to forbid truth to cry out everywhere, "Behold, here am I, admire or loathe me; honor, or spurn me, here I am." Some mutilate or distort the truth, add lies to it, misapply the eternal law, and do incredible damage. But that is aside. It is yet to be said, that it is by no man's fault the *truth* gets utterance. It is its own out speaking that makes so much clamor among men. Before the war Mr. Yancey demanded that citizens should cease to speak, as well as act, against slavery; he might as well have demanded the risen sun not to shine. A man may say the South is fighting the Abolitionists; by no means. The South fights to prove that a great principle of the New Testament ought not to assert itself among a Christian people. As though should they be victorious in every battle, truth would any the more learn to be silent. It was not the misdirected zeal of any number of men that raised the alarm, but the self-asserting power of truth, shining through disguises and bad passions, and sending beams, even in that way, from the throne of God into the slave-pen and the cotton-field.

Furthermore, truth is always antagonistical, more or less, to the prevailing order of things. In other words, there are always errors, and corrupt usages in society. To declare the truth, therefore, is to *attack* false opinion and wrong doing, and in such a way also, as to utterly destroy them. In some circumstances right opinion, uttered in a right spirit, like the light of heaven, by a wonderful chemistry, dissolves or materially changes many forms of wrong. Indeed this would always be the result, were the truth properly declared, and were the wrong doers simply unfortunate, and not in any measure attached to the forms of evil in which they live. As it is, however, there is collision; often sharp and determined conflict. He who holds an error, does not so easily relinquish it. He whose life is in the wrong, does not'so easily abandon his courses. The false opinion searches diligently for new supports. The false practice uses all manner of ingenuity to prepare a defense. At the approach of truth, therefore, the hold of sin becomes a strong hold; and intricate and massive barriers bid defiance, and the war fairly begins. Resources are husbanded on either side, and henceforth there is only a momentary lull in the fight.

Truth, when she first appears, is usually esteemed a usurper, a destructionist, reckless of domestic quiet and order, or a vaporing knight-errant, proposing quixotic adventures. In a little while the weight of her mailed hand begets a measure of respect. In a little while her patient siege and slow advances increase her honor. A few more blows, and the enemy is divided. The mere vassals of the enemy come over to the side of Right. And after a while the terms she offers are, as though for the first time, discovered to be reasonable, and we capitulate to her, in whom we were too blind to see our true sovereign and rightful Lord. It took time, waste, hard usage, perhaps blood, to open our eyes to that whose excellence we wonder we had never seen before. Such battle and siege go on in every man's life. By the same order of things the world refuses to accept righteousness till it has first poured out its blood.

The *character* of opposers makes conflict inevitable.

There are the *malignants,* who hate all that is good, who boil with rage, whenever the calm face of virtue shines out upon them,— spirits in league with hell, utterly given over to devils, so that by a natural law, they go into spasms whenever a beam from the heavenly world falls on their souls. They are the revilers, the blasphemers. They belong to the class of men who struck Jesus in the face, always the more enraged as goodness shows itself to be goodness, without the mixture of sin. These constitute an element in opposition to the progress of opinion seemingly terrific, and yet less harmful by far than the seeming.

There are also the *secularists*, those whose opposition to right is grounded mainly in personal interests; who have, it may be, no lack of admiration for abstract virtue, but at the same time have no scruples in putting aside all claims that infringe, in any way, upon their ease, or pride, or material advantage. They do not go out of their way to make war on any good thing. They do not always resent the approach of truth, unless it be clothed with power. But when their personal interests are threatened, when truth begins to undermine their caste, or their fortunes, they subsidise all their power to resist her progress. With them everything is at stake, and they make the most determined and relentless war.

There are the*purblind,* those, who in morals are on a higher plane than the last; who have a certain respect and admiration for virtue, and are not without aims to do right; who, indeed, in an absolute choice between good and evil, would choose the good at a sacrifice, but who, nevertheless, are quite incapable of discerning evil in anything venerable and time-honored, or in anything sanctioned by respectable men especially if habits and customs to which they are inured are involved in the controversy. With much that, in the lighter sense of the term, is good in them, they are almost sure, when the conflict comes, to espouse the wrong. They learn to justify it by a thousand pleas, get confirmed in the belief that evil is good, and contend for it with all the devotion of persecuted and injured men.

There are *cowards*, those who living in a still higher plane, are not utterly blinded by the prejudices of their place and time, or by personal considerations, who nevertheless, go over to the side of the wrong, through lack of real moral courage. The evil is an evil, they do most freely allow, but they see no way of escape from it. All remedies are empirical. All measures against, are fanatical. All who disapprove in strong terms, are arrogant, self-righteous intermeddlers. We are involved, they say, in that which, would to God never had a beginning,, but so it is with us; so it must be. When, therefore, truth, refusing to be silent, declares that nothing is inevitable except the past, and sets

men at decided odds with the wrong, they see greater wrong in whatever remedy than in the evil itself, and naturally wheel into line with those who are pledged to spare no pains in the defense of iniquity.

There are *the laggards*, who rising yet higher than these, mean, as God shall help them, to overthrow all customs and opinions contrary to his law. But unfortunately they put off the time of beginning so long, in hope of more favorable auspices, that the golden hour is lost. Difficulties multiply. New and complicated questions arise. Spectators, with or without an appreciation of their position, call them laggards, prophecy to them that the evil always wax worse and worse, and bid them go on. After that, all measures are an affront to them. No men, after that, are wise but they. And because truth will not wait for them; because, God is raising up children to Abraham from the stones of the street; because the day comes before they were ready for it, they will have no part in the aggression. And more, they go over to the enemy, add moral power to a bad cause, and render the conflict still more bitter and relentless.

Conflict is made necessary, also, by the *disagreements* of men who are equally impelled by the love of truth and righteousness. They have different theories, infused more or less with their own prejudices and passions. Some would never waste a word in persuasion, but attack and demolish in the least possible time; while others think right methods and a right spirit to be of as much importance as a formal victory. Some would strike the first blow at the root; while others would rather hedge in, and stifle the wrong, and others still would send in a new life to outgrow the evil, and absorb all the vital currents. Hence wars preliminary to, and attendant upon, the great war; sometimes productive of nothing but bad blood; sometimes working out the truth, that neither of the parties were wise, and ending in some great event, which shows that God needs none of them, and will set the battle in array as no man thought of beforehand.

It would be unjust not to add, that there are often parties on the right side of a given question who are so palpably on the wrong side of other questions, that they exasperate the abettors of the evil at hazzard, and afford them a seeming justification. Some men who espouse a right opinion, arc so utterly devoid of common sense, and charity, that a devil even might think it piety in him to oppose them; much more, men who are far from being abandoned. Some men, many men, who are on the right side of grave questions, are there palpably without conscience. They are valorous and virtuous, because all their worldly interests are on that side. Or they are valorous and unvirtuous, because to embrace a doctrine which demands no sacrifice *for them*, is a cheap way of maintaining self-esteem.

And still further: When we reflect how great changes a truth sometimes must needs make, if it be acknowledged, it is no longer a wonder that it unsheaths the sword. When our Lord said, "I am the Way, the Truth and the Life," he uttered words which, if true, must necessarily shake down the whole fabric of Judaism, and render *effete* the traditions of a thousand years. When the early Christians repeated his words in the streets of Rome, they demanded, in effect, that Paganism should disappear, and the Law-giver of nations should change her laws. When John Huss sounded out the word, "God so loved the world, that he gave his only begotten Son, that WHOSOEVER believeth on him might not perish," he uttered a truth, which if received, must needs abolish the priesthood and monastic orders, and the whole machinery and social life of the Church of Rome. When the English Puritan declared that God gave him the right to worship according to the dictates of his own conscience, he demanded a change in the structure of the whole kingdom. When Roger Williams declared the same thing in Massachusetts, he demanded a change in the whole structure of that Commonwealth. When the Fathers of the Republic declared, with one consent, that all men are born *free* they meant to demand of the generations after them a change, which they did not think it wise to attempt, in the civil life and domestic institutions of all the States whose foundations they had laid. These are the utterances that unsheathed the sword in Judea, in Rome, in Bohemia, in England, and in our once happy but now bloodstained land.

Take the last and to us now all-absorbing illustration. Whether the negro be equal or not to another man, (which need not be asserted nor denied) suppose him to be *born free*, having the natural right to liberty and the pursuit of happiness. Suppose it to be a demand of the New Testament that these rights be accorded to him, and how great the changes that must be made, in order to fulfil this command. Political balances must be disturbed. New industries must be established; new commercial enterprises devised and fostered. Ease and affluence must change hands, and the whole domestic life and habit of thought take new form on an area far greater than that of some of the proudest empires of the world. Consider, now, the disinterestedness and personal sacrifice necessary in order to accept such a revolution, the extraordinary virtue that must characterize not only the few but the many to make such a revolution even tolerable to them. Consider that the just and kind-hearted men and women disposed to listen to considerations of mercy, see in their own servants, a group of helpless, dependent, and yet happy people, to change whose lot, even for the better, must necessarily bring an interim of want and sorrow to both master and slave,—and who shall be found to begin in good earnest so great a work? To sum all, consider that every earthly motive suggests the putting off the day, and that on the other hand, every inducement to emancipation is an inducement of simple righteousness, unaided by worldly considerations, and besides holds out the prospect of labor and want and trouble; and we have little occasion to wonder, that a people, no worse than others, should themselves become bond slaves to this gilded lie. Nay more, consider that the great masses of any people are incapable of extraordinary sacrifices for the sake of principle *unless they have some interest in the principle,* and it ceases to be a matter of wonder that, the world demanding this millennial virtue at the hands of slaveholders, they should dream of a republic with slavery for the corner stone.

Meantime that New Testament law, that assertion of the Declaration of Independence, that love of liberty which all men possess, do not wait for difficulties to dissolve, for men to find time and convenience to disentangle their affairs, and the words boom on; the irresistible conflict comes to be a fixed war of opinion, till alas! alas I the nine millions of the South, smarting under the frown of the world, and partly conscious of the desert of that frown, dash themselves against the government; and there is no arbiter but the sword I Fire, pestilence, desolated homes and blood, must settle controversy, and widowed and wailing hearts must pay the price I

It ought to be added, that the mother crime of the South was not that her people were a slave-holding people, but that they grew into *a love* for their peculiar institutions, repented of their confessions; that her Divines prophesied falsely, and all together, they *renounced the thought of any change,* earlier or later, in their domestic institutions. Hence the necessity of the arbitrament of force, God suffering them to choose the sword. It ought also to be distinctly understood, that *they* chose the sword; *they,* not *toe.* Whatever errors we may have committed; however little the merit of our easy righteousness, requiring them to do justice to the bondman, we, at least, are permitted to remember, that we never dreamed for a moment of using the sword, or even attempting to change their laws: that it was no fault of ours, that we were able, without sacrifice, to believe the truth, the reception of which required sacrifice on their part; that we were as bounden to accept the truth and declare it, and maintain it in the national domain, as though it affected our own, as well as their, civil polity and domestic life. We are permitted to remember, that we could hardly believe in their determination to resort to arms; that we fondly dreamed that the first outbreak of rebellion was a spasm of rage, to which reason and quiet would succeed; and that we were slow to gird ourselves for anything more than a momentary conflict. *They* chose the sword. Our love of country, our sense of responsibleness to the past and to the future, and our perception that the great day had come for the trial of our national life, constrained us to accept the arbitration of the sword. We saw before us fields white with the bones of men, and watered by rivers of blood. We saw in vision, a great army of widows and orphans and mutilated men. We saw also, how far off we could not tell, a nation mightier, purer, and more glorious, emerging from the conflict, and we accepted the arbitration of the sword.

The price of our inheritance is *blood;* who shall pay the price? A great principle of the crucified Redeemer has stirred the hatred and desperation of men; the question whether the truth of God shall be silent is to be settled in blood; who shall offer himself for his country and his God?

Our husbands and brothers and sons have answered these questions. The brave and the good have leaped into the breach, and by thousands have gone down to death for ns. That a thoughtless multitude, lured only by the fascination or wages of war, have made themselves soldiers for us, does not change the fact, nor lessen its sublimity, that a great moral necessity was laid upon men, and that multitudes have given themselves to their country, as the one great duty and privilege of their lives. Their names are written in heaven, and their honor will be celebrated here, till the story of the Great Rebellion is forgotten among men.

Courage! all men! citizens I soldiers! rulers! mourners! This, great day is one of the days of the Son of Man! The Prince of Peace is hewing his way to the day of universal peace.

It is appointed unto men once to die. Each man's death illustrates some law of God's government among men. I knew of no better way of honoring the memory of our cherished friend, and fellow-believer, than by enunciating the law by which he offered his life for his country. Truth gets her charter from God, but, sorrowful to say, her seal is blood. This he knew full well. With this distinct thought in his mind, he harnessed himself for the war, as one who believed its battle-fields were altars, and who thought seriously that in the election of God's sovereignty he might be among the offerings.

JOHN A. BROSS was born in Milford, Pike county, Pennsylvania, February 21st, 1826. At the conclusion of a thorough Academic course, he engaged in the study of law, first in Goshen, New York, and afterwards in this city, where he continued in the honorable and successful practice of his profession, until he enlisted in the volunteer army of the Republic. He came to Chicago in 1848. In 1856, he was married to Miss Isabella A. Mason, daughter of Hon. Nelson Mason, now of Sterling in this State. The fruits of this union were three children, one of whom only, a little boy, four years old, survives to inherit the honor of his father's virtues.

Possessed of a calm and conscientious mind, he was one to whom the outbreaking of the rebellion would naturally suggest the question of personal duty. Rarely, if ever, yielding to mere prejudice, he was one who would naturally get insight into the issues of the contest, and devote himself understanding to the salvation of his country. Slow

to entertain new theories, undemonstrative, and unaffected, as some are, by the mere enthusiasm which new events of magnitude are calculated to inspire, he was one who, having settled a question, would henceforth have no doubts, but go on without vascillation, to the object before him. He did not respond to the first call for volunteers. He was, as we learn, weighing the question. But after serious reverses to our armies, and when it became clear that sacrifice must be made for the national honor, he saw before him but one path of duty, and gave himself without reserve to his country.

He raised a company in the 88th Illinois, otherwise the Second Board of Trade Regiment, of which he was made Captain. He had experience under fire at the battle of Perryville, where he conducted himself with great coolness and bravery. He had a conspicuous and honorable post in the battle of Stone River, in which, during the first day's fight, his regiment alone repulsed, once and again, a whole brigade. His next engagement was at the battle of Chickamauga, where, with his fellows in arms, he held the left of the right wing firm in that terrible onslaught, till they were ordered to fall back to those who had been driven by the enemy.

Other fields of labor and peril were in reserve for him, in which he displayed great capacity as an organizer and as a military leader.

The question of employing negro troops had been agitated. Prejudice against an unfortunate race caused many to doubt the wisdom of employing an Anglo-African force. Besides the doubters were many opposers. The white troops would not fight with black soldiers. The black troops would not fight at all. Black troops would be guilty of gross outrages on which war even must frown. All which meant that nothing was to be done, or allowed, which, by implication, admitted the worth of the Anglo-African as a man. "With white blood enough in him to de-Africanize him, he is yet to have no share in a war in whose issues are involved, largely, the destinies of his race. It is not safe that the stuff of which slaves are made should have any other than a menial share in the works and achievements of men. Never did an African god on the banks of the Gaboon hold more unlimited sway over the African mind, than the idea of the *inviolability of African destiny*, held over all men, even in the North, who had loved American slavery. Prejudice, however, gave way in a measure. It was remembered, that black troops fought well in the West Indies. It was remembered, that Washington used them to advantage. It was remembered, that Packenham brought a regiment of them with him to the attack on New Orleans. It was remembered, that Andrew Jack- son had black troops behind his entrenchments, and complimented them as good soldiers. Other things were remembered, and—black troops were mustered into the service of the Federal Union. They fought well, and they run—at times, just as Frenchmen and Englishmen and Yankees run. They died on the battle-field like other men. They filled as large a grave.

Mr. Bross received commission as Lieutenant Colonel, and was ordered to raise a regiment of colored troops in this State. Owing to tardy action in Illinois, and consequently the removal of large numbers of colored men, and their enlistment elsewhere, it was a difficult task. Colonel Bross succeeded, and after some months of camp drill, he was ordered to join the Ninth Army Corps under Burnside, going no one knew whither. They found themselves in the front, at Petersburg. Little dreamed they of the fate which was in store for them. Colonel Bross, however, knew his peculiar exposure, and had counted the cost. He knew that black troops would be used with less than the ordinary scrupulousness, in drawing fire of the enemy. He knew that the utmost severity would be visited upon the officers of colored troops who should fall into the hands of the enemy. Fort Pillow was before his eyes. Just before he left Chicago for Washington, I remarked upon his exposure. He replied with great seriousness, the moisture gathering in his eyes, I have counted the cost, and I am ready to be offered! I said aloud, "God bless you." I said in my heart, "Here is a Christian hero, worthy of any age or any conflict!"

The 30th of July came; a day not soon to be forgotten, even after other struggles in this war have passed out of mind. The mines were sprung. Into that horrid gap, and upon the works beyond, seven colored regiments were thrown, his among the rest. SOME ONE HAD BLUNDERED. They received no support, and fell in scores at the hand of the enraged enemy. Colonel Bross was at the head of his men in the onset; in the retreat he was in their rear, last of them all, holding aloft the battle flag. Before the remnant could escape, he received a shot in the head, and crying out "o! Lord," he instantly expired. His grave, doubtless, is the grave of those who fell that day within the line? of the enemy. God will keep his dust, and his memory will grow brighter and brighter in that long catalogue of heroes and martyrs who have given their lives to liberty and to God. It is a little remarkable that he was accustomed to repeat Tennyson's "Charge of the Light Brigade," and especially these verses:

Mr. Bross was a good husband, a tender father, a kind and generous neighbor.

He was also an humble and decided follower of Jesus. His serious attention to the claims of religion was arrested, he used to say, by the fact that his father, with whom he was going to church on a certain occasion, stopped in a lonely place to pray.

I have reason to know, that in the army he was constant in his religious duties, and in circumstances where it required no little degree of moral courage to acknowledge his convictions, and do his duty. He had, however, no cant about him. He was simply straightforward and conscientious.

He was a faithful and much-loved member of this Church. Many of us have known him long and well. Quiet, unpretentious, liberal according to his means, genial in spirit, and ready for every good word and work, we could not fail to esteem him, nor regret his loss when he left us for the field of strife. And now we mourn him, as we mourn good men whose lives have been linked with ours and are no more. Nay, as we mourn good men who die for us. Nor we alone. He has numbered himself with those for whom a nation mourns, and over whose fate the lovers of our country, in all lands, will drop a tear.

We live in solemn times. Many are strong to die. A great company of tender women wring out of their bleeding hearts, an " Amen" to God's visitation of sorrow, if there be hope, that those who live, will prove pure and great enough to maintain the heritage on whose altars their beloved are already offered. May God give us grace to be worthy of those who stand in the breach, and so inspire ns with wisdom, and the spirit of self-sacrifice, that nothing on our part may be wanting to finish the work, and that we may have some tolerable claim to share in the fruits of this time of sorrow. May God, in his mercy, give victory to our arms; turn the hearts of our enemies, and bring these days of national trial and domestic anguish to a speedy end. May God, in his mercy, give us repentance, that there may be no let nor stay to the outflow of his great compassion. May we all learn that life is not in length of days, but in deeds; that an early grave found in the service of our country and of God, is better than a long life of self-indulgence; that he who dies with uplifted arm against iniquity, dies not, but becomes immortal!

PROCEEDINGS OF THE CHICAGO BAR

RESOLUTIONS, SPEECHES, ETC.

IMMEDIATELY after it was known in the city that Colonel Bross had fallen before Petersburgh on the fatal 30th of July, a meeting of the Chicago Bar was held, and a committee was appointed to draft resolutions expressive of the sentiments of his former professional, associates. The report of the committee and the subsequent meeting was delayed for a few days, with the hope that his remains might be recovered and brought to this city for interment. Those efforts proved entirely fruitless, for, as stated in the Memorial, he was buried inside of the rebel lines, and they are still (March, 1865,) in their possession. His friends now have little hope that they will ever be able to find his resting place. On Thursday, August 18tli, one of the most deeply affecting and solemn meetings ever convened by the Chicago Bar, was held at the rooms of the Law Institute. As remarked by one of the speakers, they had lost one over whose character no mantle of charity need be thrown—in regard to whose life and death there was nothing to conceal. The first three or four speeches are given as reported in the CHICAGO TRIBUNE of the next day. The others have been kindly furnished for this Memorial by those who made them. The chair was occupied by "WM. A. PORTER, ESQ., and G. PAYSON was elected Secretary.

GEORGE HERBERT, ESQ., the chairman OF the Committee appointed on Resolutions, reported the following

RESOLUTIONS

WHEREAS, Our friend and brother, Lieutenant Colonel JOHN A. BROSS, 29th regiment U. S. Colored Troops, has fallen upon the field of battle—another victim upon the altar of our country,

Resolved, That by his glorious death this Bar has lost one of its most cherished members, his regiment an able and fearless commander, the country a bravo soldier, and humanity an earnest advocate and uncompromising friend. While wo mourn, we cannot but gather consolation that another of our number, (having courageously assumed the chances alike from an open enemy in honorable warfare, and a malignant foe in indiscriminate massacre,) ripe in Christian character and manly virtue, and impelled by patriotic devotion, has thus enrolled his name on that long list of heroes enshrined in the hearts of a grateful nation.

Resolved, That though we shall miss Colonel Bross in the halls of justice and in the other walks of our common profession, we shall not cease to remember the urbanity of his deportment, the geniality of his companionship, the integrity of his purposes, and the honesty of his heart.

Resolved, That from our earliest acquaintance our departed brother illustrated the principles of universal philanthropy having their foundation in the gospel he professed; and while his military career gave the highest evidence of his self-sacrificing patriotism and his fidelity to early convictions, leading him to seek a path of danger unequaled in civilized warfare, in his heroic death he has sealed with his blood those great principles of our common humanity, which he believed to be inculcated by his Divine Master.

Resolved, That we do not and will not forget that the dearest and tenderest of ties bound Colonel Dross to family, home and earth, and increased the sacrifice thus cheerfully made at the shrine of principle, patriotism, and humanity, and that we tender to those he held most dear our cordial sympathy in this bereavement.

Resolved, That a suitable committee be appointed to communicate the above resolutions to the United States Courts and the several courts of record, with the request that they be recorded therein.

Resolved, That copies of the foregoing resolutions, signed by the Chairman and Secretary, be presented to the family and brothers of the deceased, as a testimonial of sympathy and regard.

REMARKS OF MR. HERBERT.

In moving the adoption of the resolutions, GEORGE HERBERT, ESQ., spoke nearly as follows:

When I see around me the preceptor, the fellow-students, those who have stood on the same battle-field, and those who have been more intimately associated with Colonel Bross, in the work of doing good in the same church, I hardly feel entitled, as the mere professional brother and friend, to occupy your time, but overruled by the opinions of others, I will follow the impulses of my heart.

On similar occasions I have ordinarily been silent, not from any want of sympathy with the object, but our profession has been so careful that the good our deceased brothers do, should not "be interred with their bones," and in their friendly zeal they have illustrated with such signal success, the heathen maxim—*Nihil de mortuin nisi bonutn—*

that my simple English would sound tame and out of place. What, however, throws special interest upon this gathering is, that words and empty adjectives are not wanted to add to the simple, truthful homage to a deceased brother, friend, patriot, soldier, and Christian.

If our friend and brother were now here present, and could he give direction to our thoughts and words, he would not have us mention, as his most enduring claim upon our sympathy, esteem and remembrance, his standing in our profession, however honorable, his sacrifices for his country, however noble and patriotic, or his courage, or even the circumstances of his death; but the fact that he had ever lived an honest, sincere, upright, Christian life; that he had acted well his part, and when tried in the even balances, not of professional charity, but of gospel candor, he had not been found wanting.

My knowledge of Colonel Bross was not so early in life as that of many others, neither do I feel that I have the same right to speak of him in his domestic and inner life as his more intimate associates. When I knew him, the heyday of youth was past. He was then just engaging in the earnest pursuits of his profession with all the strength of early manhood, and was forming around him those social bonds and family ties now so rudely sundered. Our intercourse was ever most cordial, our companionship was most genial, and beside the ordinary bond of professional brotherhood, there was another link between us never unrecognized.

I shall confine my remarks to but a single view of Colonel Brass' character, as the same has seemed illustrated in the last three years of his life, and leave to others whom I see around me to enlarge on its symmetrical proportions as developed in every relation he sustained to his family, to society, the bar, the church, and the nation. You all know his industry, his urbanity, his genial spirit, his integrity, his sense of professional honor, and the truthfulness of his unostentatious life. But few, however, if any, even among his professional brethren or his intimate friends, would have supposed with his modest mien he could rise to distinction in civil life, much less in military. Yet beneath that calm exterior lay a mine of feeling hid from the public gaze, and an element of power which could, upon occasion, elevate him to the highest round of patriotic devotion and heroism, and nerve him for great deeds.

"While the heroic Roberts could by his commanding and massive presence, his dashing boldness, and the power of his will, control mankind and command our admiration, and, without fear and without reproach, court death in every charge—while the gallant and eloquent Mulligan, in the demonstrative enthusiasm of his paternity, at the right time and the right place might speak words which having uttered he might well afford to die; it has been left to the no less gallant and bold, though less impulsive and enthusiastic Bross, to give a dying testimonial to the sincerity of his convictions, the ardor of his patriotism and the self-sacrificing principles of his all-absorbing philanthropy.

Roberts, at the first ring of battle, the first clash of arms, springs to the fore front of the affray; Mulligan, at the first roar of cannon from Sumter, rushes forth among his countrymen, and by his impulsive nature and his eloquence, communicated his own enthusiasm, and with burning words enlists their aid. Both died characteristically, true to their instincts and the great impelling influences of their respective lives. Nor was Bross less true to his own manhood and the controlling influences of his own character. More phlegmatic, less ardent, less demonstrative, but not less patriotic, nor less brave, he did not seek on the first impulse and upon the excitement of the moment, the storm of battle; but watching the great conflict which in his mind soon assumed vast proportions, and involved those great principles of civilization and humanity which he had long held dear, and which had become a part of his own nature, upon the second call for troops, having deliberately, and we doubt not prayerfully, counted the cost, as a matter of patriotic duty and individual sacrifice,, he engaged in the arduous conflict.

I see those around me who have stood with him on the same battle-field, and can testify to his worth as a soldier, and an officer, and here mingle as professional brothers, their regrets with ours over his death.

Colonel Bross entered the army in the 88th Illinois, for which he enlisted a company, leaving this city in August, 1862. The campaigns of Kentucky and Tennessee brought him practically into direct contact with an element in the great contest, which before he had studied theoretically only at a distance. His conviction of the great fact that *"God had made of one blood all the nations to dwell upon all the face of the earth,"* had early been with him a settled principle of faith; and when the Government decided to call forth that great element of power representing four millions of our population, and give them their position as mon in this conflict, no one was surprised that Captain Bross applied for power to enlist a regiment in Illinois. In this he was measurably successful.

He needed but the maximum of a regiment to have received a commission as Colonel.

A man of less principle would have hesitated. He had as much to lose as any other man; as much to bind him to family, friends and home; as much to induce him to temporize and delay; but foremost in this State at the hazard of life—nay, though counting it almost certain death—he engaged in the effort which he believed would demonstrate the truth of the divine statement to the most unbelieving, and would elevate the chattel to the full rank of manhood, and disabuse a public sentiment which he looked upon not only as a reproach upon our State and nation, but upon our common Creator.

Colonel Bross entered on this work with an enthusiasm lighted up by patriotism, philanthropy and religion. With him the great brotherhood of man had its foundation in a common Creator, a common ancestry, and a common destiny, and anything that practically denied that, was to him infidelity.

I shall ever remember the magnetic grasp of his hand, and the earnest fervor of his mild and determined eye, when he bade me his last farewell. His manner, indeed the whole man impressed me with the feelings from that moment, that John A. Bross would return, if ever, a dead man or a hero. You all know the result. On the 30th of July, before Petersburgh, on the parapet of the enemy, planting the flag of the country—the flag he so much loved—he fell, covered with the folds of that flag and with glory, and attested the sincerity of his faith and his philanthropy, by mingling his blood with that of the despised and oppressed race whose welfare and whose elevation he sought with so much earnestness and zeal!

It was fitting to live such a life—it was glorious to die such a death.

Our country had been so long at peace, and false notions of honor and chivalry and personal courage had been left so long without practical contradiction, that the majority among us had ignored the lessons of history, and had divorced the ideas of personal courage and heroism from the milder virtues of religion, and had forgotten that the most striking illustrations of these attributes had been connected with high religious fervor and enthusiasm.

If the ancients wished to stimulate the Greek, they spoke of his household gods. If they wished to inspire the valor of the Roman, they promised him immortal honors with the heroes of antiquity. If they would urge on the stubborn Jew, they spoke of the altar and the temple—the graves of the prophets and the great Jehovah.

It was this feeling of religious enthusiasm which moved the sword of the Lord and of Gideon; which nerved the arm of the youthful David to hurl the smooth stone from the brook; that stimulated the infant Hannibal; that beamed in the fervid eye of the Maid of Orleans; that sustained the patient courage of Washington. This it was which in our own day gave England her Havelock, and has among ourselves raised up the idols of our army and our navy—our Foote and our Howard—and is now developing a host of minor worthies, each of whom, if not enrolled high in the annals of fame, will be found registered in the hearts of his comrades, and in that great catalogue of Christian martyrs and heroes in the Lamb's book of life.

This great principle is most happily illustrated in the life and death of Colonel Bross. His death, like his life, was the development of a calm and patient pursuit of what he thought a religious duty. "He loved his fellow-men," and thus attested by the divine law, his love for his country and to his God.

If, when surrounded by home and by friends—

"The chamber where the good man meets his fate Is privileged beyond the common walk Of virtuous life, quite in the verge of Heaven,"

how near to the great white throne above must be that favored spot of earth where, heralded by the thunders of battle and canopied by the smoke and flame of contending armies, with one hand on the flag, the same Christian hero and martyr, with heart full of love for his country, his brother, and his God, yields up his life, and whence his released spirit takes its flight to the bosom of that God who "is no respecter of persons," but of whom it is said that "in every nation he that feareth God and worketh righteousness is accepted with him."

But there is another picture. My courage fails me; I would fain stop. I, too, at the age of four years, was the orphan son; my mother, now eight}" years of age, was the widowed mother. I can well remember these long years of orphanage, in which there was no father's hand between me and the cold charities of an unfeeling world. I but too well remember those long years of widowhood, and of loneliness, and I can also recollect the consolation with which, even to this day, expressions of sympathy for the living and respect for the dead, like those before us, are treasured up as the green spots in the desert of the past. I need not urge you, my brethren, in your memory of the dead not to forget the living, or to cherish them as the nearest link on earth to bind us to our departed brother in Heaven—nor need I to enjoin upon you the duty to commend them to the widow's God and the father of the fatherless.

REMARKS OF HON. GRANT GOODRICH.

Hon. GRANT GOODRICH, in seconding the motion to adopt the resolutions, remarked that he could not let the opportunity pass without paying a tribute to the memory of one whom he knew long and respected greatly. In 1850, Colonel Bross entered his office as a student of law, and after years of close study, left it to commence the battles of life. His virtues were well known to all who were honored by his friendship. He was faithful as a student, and successful as a practitioner. In his private life he was a slave to no vice, and was almost a perfect model of manhood. All who knew him well, speak of him with feelings of respect and affection. While they, his professional brethren, mourn his death, there is mingled with their sorrow, a feeling of pride that another member of their profession has distinguished himself as a soldier patriot. The law has ever been the champion of freedom and the guardian of liberty. In the old English Revolution there exists a bright galaxy of names of members of the bar whose patriotism has given to their names imperishable fame; and later, in our own Revolution, many of the profession were called upon to leave the halls of justice for the battle-field. Our very Constitution was the handiwork of the law, and the old Declaration of Independence was the production of a lawyer. The members before him have, on several occasions, been called upon to mourn the loss of those who had gone out in the defense of freedom and free institutions, but deep as their sorrow may be, they know the glorious cause of their departure, and do not mourn as those without hope.

All men, the eloquent speaker continued, should live for an aim—a purpose; and if on their deathbed they can feel that the world is better for their life,

they have not lived in vain; and whether they fall in the civil strife, of everyday life, struggling for influence, distinction or fame, or whether they fall nobly upon the field of battle, they have accomplished the end of life. Of the two ends, how much more sublime is that of the warrior who has fallen for the right. An imperishable halo of glory surrounds his name, which the highest and noblest civil exploits could never impart. How much would every one before me wish that his sire had died the death of a patriot soldier hero, upon the battle-field. "With what feelings of pride would the son of such a father take his child upon his knee, and instill into its young mind feelings of holy veneration for the heroic dead, and the cause for which he offered up his life.

It therefore behoves the Bar to rejoice that the death of Colonel Bross was in this manner, if die he must. In such a death another thought is involved. It is the highest duty of men to attempt to imitate the Saviour of humanity, in his earthly life. He died that his blood might be a ransom for many, to bind up the hearts of the broken-hearted, and disseminate universal liberty to the oppressed. Now there are national sins, as well as individual transgressions, and the crime of a nation can no more be expiated without the shedding of blood than those of a single human being; so that he who in dying atones for the sins of his country, falls nearer the standing point of his Redeemer than any other man. As a nation, the speaker was certain, we had sinned grievously; we had given ourselves up to the pursuit of pleasure and of luxuries, and had been careless regarding the high and exalted ends of our national prosperity. He believed that had America gone on for the next forty years as she had for the last forty, she would have been utterly lost, and in her destruction freedom would have been subverted and destroyed. But it was wisely ordained that this state of affairs was not to be. War purifies the political heavens in the same manner that the thunder storm purifies the atmosphere, and the world feels purer and stronger for the struggle.

The noble Bross has fallen for us, and we feel safer and securer at home; but it is because the bayonets of patriots are a wall of death between them and the foe; and were it not for such men as the noble dead, our streets would be overrun with rebel hordes, who would destroy our civil and religious rights.

Though, as Mr. Goodrich justly remarked, the departed has left a widowed wife and orphan child, yet, in the consciousness that their husband and father has fallen in the exercise of his highest duties, there is a consolation which the greatest anguish cannot destroy. We, his professional brothers, mourn his death, but why do we mourn? Colonel Bross occupies a higher position than he or his hearers could ever attain, unless they follow in his glorious footsteps.

In conclusion the speaker continued: A day will come when on every battlefield of this impious rebellion, a marble monument will be erected, on which the names of the gallant fallen shall be inscribed, and round which their children and children's children will drop a tear for the memory of their country's deliverers, and plant sweet flowers to perfume the hallowed spot. Until this marble shall be destroyed in the last convulsion, those names will be imperishably remembered, while ours will pass out of remembrance.

The thought of this probability should inspire the Union arms with fresh strength, each man determining that these sacred spots where bravo men fell shall be wrested from rebel hands, so that loyal hearts and loyal hands can pay a suitable tribute to the departed without being prevented by a foreign despotic nationality, which the South is attempting to establish. [4]

REMARKS OF MAJOR STEVENSON.

The meeting was next addressed by Major ALEX. F. STEVENSON, formerly a comrade of the deceased on the battle-field. He said:

I should prefer to be a silent mourner. And still when I think of him whose death and loss we lament, emotions begin to arise in my heart which compel me to speak as a feeling of duty to him we shall see no more, and to the widow and child who have looked upon the beloved form of the husband and father for the last time on this earth. Well may they weep. Well may you, my brethren of this Bar, look sad. Well may Chicago be robed again in mourning, and well may the flag on this Court House again be unfolded to the breeze of Heaven at half-mast, for another hero has departed, and another patriot has sacrificed himself upon the altar of his country. But he rests in peace. You who have assembled here this day to pay the last customary tribute to a departed brother, you have known him as a man, a citizen, a lawyer, a Christian, and a friend; and I am here not to speak of him as such, but to bear testimony to his qualities and virtues as a soldier and a patriot. A few days before the bloody battle of Stone River, when the brigade—commanded by the gallant soldier and member of this Bar, who died too soon for his country's good, I mean Colonel Roberts—joined General Sheridan's Division, I had the pleasure of shaking hands and renewing acquaintance and friendship with Colonel (then Captain) Bross, and from thence dated my knowledge of his military career. It became my duty as Inspector General of Sheridan's Division, to keep watch and report especially upon the efficiency and conduct of officers, and I must say here, not because he is dead and I would speak in eulogy of him, but because truth compels me, that he was one of the best, most temperate and efficient officers in the division. Whenever, in my path of duty, I inspected his command, be it in the camp or on the picket line, I always found him at his post, ready to do everything that might be required of him with a cheerful spirit of willingness. No grumbling ever passed his lips; he never shirked his duty. In the rain and tempest, and under the scorching rays of a Southern sun, he lived with his men, doing his duty as a soldier and a patriot. He was not one of those men continually around his superiors begging for favors; he was humble and modest in his ways, but proud to be an American soldier. In battle there was none braver than he. At Stone River and Chickamauga, battles historic for the bravery of our troops against heavy numerical superiority of the enemy, he displayed that coolness and determination which fitted him so much for a higher command.

But it seems to me Colonel Bross had still greater moral courage than we gave him eredit for. He has shown it in taking the command of colored troops. To take this step required a man of nerve and fortitude, for he knew that to the officers of colored troops there was no imprisonment like unto others, but certain death awaited them should the chances of war cast them into the hands of the enemy. But with the full knowledge of all this, he went bravely into the contest, because he believed it to be his duty to his country and his God.

On that Saturday morning, when the first rays of the Eastern sun lighted up the flying clouds above, and the day began that might have decided not alone the fate of this nation, but of liberty itself,—when in the calm preceding the storm, there all at once arose a mountain of dust,—when the mine was sprung, and the descending masses buried rebels by the hundred, then our gallant men went forward to the charge, to dislodge, if human strength could do it, the rebels from their strong-hold. But alas, the fire of the enemy mowed them down as they advanced. At last the colored division was ordered forward, and there Colonel Bross might be seen fearlessly leading his colored' men, who desired to do their mite in this great struggle of liberty.

He fell as heroes fall, with the old flag, so dear to him, in his hand, nearest the enemy. Need I comment upon it? His acts speak louder than my words. "When this cruel war shall be over, and our glorious banner shall again wave triumphant over the whole land, the city of Chicago, I trust, will erect a monument in memory of those heroes who have gone from her midst, and have fallen on the bloody battle-fields of our country, that future generations may linger around that hallowed spot and gaze upon it with love and veneration. And among heroes like Roberts, Scott, Hall, Chandler, Mulligan, Mihalotzy, and others, let the name of John A. Bross, the brave commander of the 29th colored infantry, be placed in conspicuous characters.

REMARKS OF L. B. TAFT.

L. B. TAFT, Esq., President of the Board of Education, the next speaker, had been out of town, and had but just heard of this meeting, but desired to add his tribute to the memory of their departed brother. He said: was ever affable, courteous and kind-hearted—in fine, a model Christian. He always had a kind word for every one, true as steel to all his friends, and whenever he met those whom affliction or adversity had visited, he consoled them with words of sympathy and kindness. Once, and again, and now again, has a brother fallen in the defense of the liberties of our country. His memory will ever be embalmed in the hearts of his brethren, in the church, at the bar, among his neighbors and friends, as well as in the hearts of his countrymen.

GEORGE CHANDLER, formerly a Lieutenant in the 88th Illinois, made some feeling and eloquent remarks. He said that he had known Colonel Bross during the whole period of his service in the 88th Illinois as an active, faithful, patriotic, self-sacrificing soldier. He had stood by his side at Perryville, Stone River, Murfreesboro and Chickamauga, and no braver man could be found on those fields than. Captain Bross. He had seen him at all times and under all circumstances, but never did he, in the temptations of field or camp, compromise, for an instant, his Christian integrity. He was always the same self-sacrificing, faithful soldier, friend and Christian, and his name will be ever held in fragrant remembrance for his long list of virtues, as well as for the great sacrifices he made in life, and for his glorious death.

REMARKS OF J. H. THOMPSON.

JOHN H. THOMPSON, Esq., spoke as follows:

I have been requested by Mr. H. E. Seelye, who has long been one of the most intimate friends of Colonel Bross, to express his deep regret that he was obliged to be absent from the city on the occasion of this meeting.

It seems to me, Mr. Chairman, to be enough to say of any man that he has alien for his country, in this great struggle for the preservation of our national existence. Whatever may have been his faults or errors—and it is not for mortals to claim perfection—we may well forget them when he has atoned for them by such self-sacrifice. And whatever other virtues or merits he may have had, whatever else he may have done, which, under other circumstances, might seem worthy of praise or commendation, all seems lost in the splendor of this crowning act of heroism, patriotism and devotion.

There are many things in the life and character of our gallant brother which were worthy of praise; many things which those of us who knew him can never willingly let die from memory. He was a warm-hearted, genial and faithful friend, an upright and honorable lawyer, an active and exemplary Christian. He was a true man in every relation of life, and has gone from us leaving no stain or reproach on his name. And yet when I think of him I can think only of the soldier falling so gallantly for his country, bearing into that tempest of fire and death the flag we love, dying as a soldier would wish to die—but borne, as in a chariot of fire, from this mortal to immortal life. We need say no more than tell the simple story of how he fought and how he fell. What are our praises and eulogies beside the eloquence of such a death? Our praises will be forgotten; but deeds like these, embalmed in history, go down the centuries. The story of the hero dying for his country, old but over new, never loses its charm for the eager ear of childhood or the dimmer eyes of age.

Allusions have been made here to the numbers who have gone to the war from our profession. They have gone with unfaltering step at the call of their country, and some of them have fallen, like Colonel Bross, under circumstances of peculiar interest, and have won imperishable names in their country's history. There are tears for the vacant places in our professional ranks. There are tears for the bereaved and broken-hearted. There are tears for our country in the hour of its darkness and trial, but there is nothing for tears in a death so glorious as that of the patriot hero.

And out of these losses we may draw auguries of hope and cheer for our country and our cause. The martyr and the hero never die in vain, and it cannot be that these sacrifices have been made for naught. It cannot be that that flag which has been borne so gallantly can ever trail in dishonor. It must be that that flag for which such gallant spirits have given themselves, and towards which, in the hour of mortal anguish, the last thoughts of some of them have turned, shall yet float in triumph from every steeple and hill-top and headland, from the lakes to the gulf, and that every star on that beloved banner which has gone into dark eclipse, shall shine unclouded and undimmed.

REMARKS OF H. F. WAITE.

H. F. WAITE, Esq., said:

On this mournful occasion that has convened us together, I cannot remain silent. A brother, a patriot, and a soldier, has fallen; not in old age, but in early manhood; not at home, surrounded by the sympathy of loved ones, but upon the battle-field! amid the iron hail and leaden rain."

For thirteen years I have known Colonel Bross well. Meeting him often in the practice of our common profession, I can indorse all that has been said of him to-day. As a lawyer, he was industrious, pains-taking and careful. No client entrusted business to him without its receiving every attention, or afterwards ever regretted having done so. He brought to the discharge of his professional duties the same conscientiousness that characterized him in the other walks of life. He was a man of good judgment, and had carefully studied his profession, and was a good lawyer. He acted well his part in the performance of all his professional duties. What higher tribute can be paid to any professional man? As a citizen, he was respected and honored. As a Christian, his brethren in the church with which he was connected, bear their testimony to his noble and active Christian character. His life amid the world was in keeping with his Christian profession, as they who daily associated with him will attest. As a soldier he was brave—none braver; and he has died as a soldier loves to die. And when, as we trust and hope, "the stars and stripes" shall float where now rests his body, and when all that remains of John A. Bross is restored to us, and placed, as we trust and hope it soon will be, in one of our own cemeteries, and when a marble slab shall mark his resting-place, on it shall be inscribed, "Here lies the body of a kind husband and father; a good lawyer, a Christian gentleman, a firm friend, a brave soldier, and an excellent officer; a, patriot, who attested his love for his country by dying in the deadly breach, that the institutions and liberties which our fathers bequeathed to us maybe handed down to our children unimpaired." This inscription would not be the language of eulogy but the utterance of truth. What nobler eulogy could be desired upon any one's tombstone?

REMARKS OF HON. I. N. ARNOLD, M. C.

Hon. **ISAAC N. ARNOLD** said:

Another martyr to liberty and our country's cause has fallen, and I desire to add my tribute, with these of my brethren of the Bar, to his memory.

As a constituent, one among those noble, patriotic, self-sacrificing volunteers, of which our city has furnished so many, who gave up home and family for country, I have watched his brilliant military career with ever-increasing interest and pride from its commencement until its termination in a glorious death. It is a source of pride and satisfaction to me, to feel that I have long enjoyed his political friendship and his personal regard, and that he was ever my true and faithful friend. Indeed, his manly, steadfast, consistent character, forbade his ever being to any a mere *fair-weather* friend. Wherever he gave his confidence and friendship, there he was ever to be found, ever true and devoted.

I know the high motives which led him to engage in the raising and organization of colored troops. I had the gratification of rendering him some slight assistance in this enterprise, and I know the devoted patriotism and the unselfish regard for duty, and the heroism, which, while conscious of all the peculiar dangers in which he was likely to be involved, hesitated not a moment in what seemed to him to be the path of duty.

I remember very vividly my last interview with him. It was the Saturday before he marched from his camp, near Alexandria, to join the forces of Grant, confronting Lee. I drove over with my family from Washington to his quarters. It was a most beautiful sunny afternoon, and I saw him with great pride review his regiment on dress parade. He had received his marching orders, and was full of enthusiasm and very proud of his regiment. He assured me that in capacity for service, endurance, courage, and all the qualities of a soldier, his regiment of negroes would not be outdone by any regiment, white or black, in the service. He took a seat in my carriage and rode with mo a short distance towards Washington. I parted with him as the sun sunk behind the blue hills of Virginia, and as we shook hands in farewell, I never was more impressed by any man. He was sun-burnt and manly—his large, fine, manly form full of health and vigor, filled with the martial ardor of the soldier and the hero. He struck his tents that night—led his gallant regiment to Petersburgh, and found there the death of a hero and a martyr. I can truly say that in all the rich sacrifices of this war there has fallen not one more manly, brave and true: none more patriotic and disinterested: no more worthy *Christian soldier* than JOHN A. BROSS.

REMARKS OF.JAMES P. ROOT, ESQ.

MR. PRESIDENT: I cannot let this occasion pass without adding my testimonial to the worth, the virtue, the patriotism of our own departed brother. When one of our number departs in the ordinary way—when his dying pillow is smoothed by kind hands, and affectionate friends stand around his bed to bid him farewell, we meet to grieve over his departure while we pay tribute to his worth. But, Sir, when one of our number goes forth in defense of his country's flag to maintain its honor and glory, when he assumes command which brings with it the *double danger* of falling on the field or *being slain by a remorseless foe while their prisoner*, words are inadequate to the expression of our admiration and respect for his bravery. It is, Sir, a test of heroism and virtue when a man leaves his home, his wife and little ones, to risk the dangers of a

battle-field. But what can we say of that man who does all this, and more—who rushes to the point of danger, and while his men are falling like leaves in the autumn gale, plants the flag on the works of the enemy!

I have known Colonel Bross intimately for ten years. I have met him in the various walks of life, and I have ever esteemed him as an honored member of the Bar, a true friend and a Christian gentleman. In saying this, I am uttering words of truth, without color, without exaggeration. If these things can be said of us truthfully, then, Sir, *we have succeeded in life*. But if there is added a glorious record as a soldier and patriot, then words are unnecessary to perpetuate our memory. They will live forever. Farewell to Bross! We shall see him no more among us, for he is joined to a noble band of Christian patriots, [11] whose memories are enshrined in the hearts of their countrymen."

REMARKS OF THOMAS DENT, ESQ.

MR. CHAIRMAN: It is not necessary for me, as a friend and neighbor of our departed brother, to add a word to what has been so justly said in regard to his character and virtues in private life. He left there none but friends; and we instinctively look to the broader field into which he entered to find some consolation for his loss.

Fit as he was to participate in the victories of peace, his days were not numbered for these alone. There was in reserve for him a more conspicuous place in the roll of honor. He obeyed the impulses of his heart, and laid down his life in support of the cause he cherished. Thus has he become identified with the martyrs whose virtues are to ornament the pages of history.

Our gallant soldiers, enrolled for the protection and preservation of the Republic, represent, in nativity, all the nations of Europe, from the ice-bound shores of the North to the sunny plains of Italy. These, as freely as any born here, have proved their title to the gratitude of the country. Patriotic motives, endearing them to us, have caused them to march together in the dreaded highway of war. And, appreciating their services, is it not to be hoped that while heretofore there have been apparent diversities of interest, and many sources of separation and division between our people, this struggle may create a truer and better union of hearts and hands? The coat of many colors, after having been stained with blood, was carried to the aged patriarch to show him that the loved one was lost, and yet all was ordered for the best, so that from seeming misfortune sprang much good. Thus may not our distracted country, now rent and scarred by civil discord, be still preserved for a nobler re-union, when all may look together to the same garner-house of national life?

Colonel Bross did what he could to defend his country against the parricidal arm yet unbroken. And was it not proper, too, that one so rich in the fruitage of a good heart, should have bought with his life the honor of having assisted, in a marked degree, to inspire a fallen race with nobler thoughts and sentiments better fitting them for liberty? Nay, more, is he not to stand before their brethren in other lands, and in future times, as a self-devoted representative of the truth that the divine gift of manhood, however it may be obscured, animated the pulsations of their hearts? If it was not for them, from inward power of renovation, to lift themselves above a menial condition; yet the examples to be held before them, to guide them onward to a higher destiny, are rapidly multiplying.

He whose loss we mourn, has now, by his own choice, been placed side by side with the lamented Shaw, and others of like fame, over whose historical monuments this regeneration may spring, as Divine Wisdom, with unceasing economy of all that is her own, invigorates the soul of man. And in the place to which he was led by the providence of God, may he stand in his death, mourned as is his loss by those who cannot be comforted; and may his life be another guiding star, not only to the few who witnessed his presence here, but to many nations yet unborn.

REMARKS OF JOHN W. WAUGHOP, ESQ.

MR. CHAIRMAN: It has not been my custom, Sir, on occasions of this nature, to participate in the speaking, for the reason that others more capable of doing justice to the subject have been ready to occupy the time. But constraining impulses now bring me to my feet. On many such occasions, an effort has been made to conceal the irregularities of the lives of some of our brethren, and we have met and thrown the mantle of charity over their lives, and remembered only their endearments. But to-day we contemplate a life, which, in all the relations of friend, lawyer, Christian, gentleman, and soldier, presents a model.

There are those present who have known Colonel John A. Bross intimately as a Christian and a friend. There are those present who have known him as a lawyer practicing his profession, and there are those who have known him as a soldier; and in all these relations he was true, active and faithful. We may challenge any one who has known the lamented Colonel in any and all the relations of life, to lay aught to his charge. None knew him but to love and respect him and those who knew him *best,* loved him *most.* Colonel Bross was entirely free from all the objectionable habits of life, and was without a vice. It made no difference whether he was in the minority or in the majority, he acted for the right, and from principle; and over such a life as this we may well shed out tears, and pay our last sad tribute.

It was, however, as a soldier that the acme of his fame was attained. In this the crowning glory of his life was reached, and this latest act will cause his name to live among the heroes of this wonderful struggle. To my mind, there has been no more illustrious death in the war than that of our lamented brother. Sir, no man has a greater admiration for the Union soldier than I have, and no one holds in more grateful remembrance than I do, the memory of the illustrious dead who have fallen for their country.

The circumstances attending the death of Colonel Bross are such as have developed the highest degree of heroism, and the truest metal of human nature. Look at him leaving an honorable rank, in the line of promotion, in the 88th Illinois, and allying himself to a regiment of men who have been brought into disrepute by a cruel and wicked thraldom. This, Sir, in the midst of a perverted public opinion, was an act of bravery; but the man who assumed this command did it with a full knowledge of the fact that he would have to lead them into the thickest of the fight, with the assurance that, if captured, no quarter would be shown, and that it was almost certain death thus to contend with such a barbarous foe. Then, Sir, see the deliberation with which he prepared for the great struggle. Ordering his horse and trappings to be delivered to his wife, in case he should not come back. Then going into the deadly struggle at the head

of his command, he led them to the muzzle of the cannon and the point of the bayonet of the enemy, while one color-sergeant fell, and another, and another, and still another, when the old flag was seized by the intrepid Colonel, and borne forward with the exclamation, "Follow me, my brave boys!" when, pierced by a ball, he fell to rise no more. Could there be a more glorious death? It is an honor to have been associated with such a man.

Our ranks, as a profession, are being rapidly thinned by these splendid deaths. The sacrifice is a great one. The best men all over this country are being slain; but, Sir, if this war shall continue during the whole of our lifetime, if we all live to the common age of men, and the whole country be stripped to poverty the struggle should not be given up.

Sir, I feel that we, as a community, have a right to be proud of the career of our lamented Colonel Bross. He has passed beyond the clash of resounding arms, and beyond our adulations, and is forever at rest.

REMARKS OF J. N. BARKER, ESQ.

MR. CHAIRMAN: It has been my pleasure to have intimately known the deceased, Colonel John A. Bross, from the year 1850 till his death. I first became acquainted with him in the office of Messrs. Morris & Goodrich, when we were both pursuing our legal studies, and from that time on, we were bound together by strong bonds of friendship. I knew him after he had finished his course of study and had opened his office for practice. Our business relations were closely connected, each of us having a considerable practice in the admiralty court, and in this way I saw much of him. I knew him in the close relations of life. As a friend I could appreciate his warmth of heart—his true and disinterested friendship, his nobleness of nature. I knew him as a Christian gentleman, and no man ever saw anything in the life of John A. Bross to cause a reproach to be brought upon the profession of Christianity.

He was a benevolent man—giving wherever he saw an object of charity, even more than his ability would justify.

He was a true patriot. From the firing of the first gun on Sumter, he entered into this war with the true spirit of patriotism, aiding in the raising of men and money, and setting his own house in order that he might go himself. Colonel Bross often, in conversation with me, lamented his inability to go at once.

As a student he was always true to his own manhood and the interests of his preceptor and employer. As a lawyer, he was a good counsellor, and no client ever had reason to regret placing his business in his hands. He was faithful and competent. As a friend he could always be relied on, and no man who enjoyed his friendship ever doubted him. As a Christian gentleman, none stood higher than he; he was foremost in every good word and work. To know him was to love him. Wherever duty called, John A. Bross wasalways to be found.

May our record of life be as fair as his.

REMARKS OF H. B. UURD, ESQ.

"MR. CHAIRMAN: There is a pleasure though mournful indeed, in talking over in this familiar way, the cherished recollections of our deceased brother, Colonel Bross, and although the remarks of my brethren have been protracted to a considerable length, yet I feel that I shall not weary you in adding my humble tribute to his memory. What you have said of his high Christian and professional character and faithful friendship does not fall upon my ear, only, as merited praise, but it finds response in my heart, as one who has been a recipient of their grateful fruits. I have had the pleasure of an intimate acquaintance with the deceased since he first came to this city, and know by experience, of his kindness, that what you have said of him is true, and it gives me great pleasure to dwell upon these his qualities; but we are attracted from these recollections to the part he has acted in the great national struggle. One of the important questions involved in this great contest is, "Shall the slave be elevated to liberty?" and in this question is involved another, "How shall he be fitted for freedom?" All history teaches us that every people who would be free and fitted to enjoy freedom, must themselves fight for it, and lay their own sacrifices of blood upon its altar. They must have a history of heroic deeds and shrines of heroes slain. The people of this oppressed and despised race have willingly and wisely accepted these conditions. Trusting in our pledged faith, they have asked to be led into the great struggle. In accepting their offered services, it has become necessary that they should be officered by men who are not only capable of leading them to battle, but of bringing out those better and higher qualities of their nature which shall fit them for the enjoyment of liberty—such men as have been accustomed to labor with true Christian love and zeal for the welfare of the poor and despised. Such a man was our lamented brother. And I feel grateful to him for his noble example. Not a few among us cease not to add their discouragements and obloquy to the terror of the rebels' threat of certain death to all officers of negro soldiers. Yet in the face of this, and with his well-established character for bravery and military capacity, which would have commanded for him high honors, he placed himself at their head, and seizing the blessed flag of his country, he led them to the deadly strife.

"When such as bear the highest honor of professional and Christian life become their leaders and standard bearers, and when they will follow them in the face of certain death, can there be a doubt of the ultimate elevation of the slave? Is it not a reason of confidence both to them and to us?

If ever we shall be permitted to visit that battle ground where Colonel Bross so nobly fell, and pay our homage to our brave brothers who there died for our country and for us, we shall meet that now despised and oppressed people there. They have patriotic blood spilt there, and their brothers sleep with ours; and he shall have double homage—the gratitude of his fellow-citizens whose country is saved, and of the freedman who has been redeemed from slavery. It will be our common shrine, or it will be an enemy's country.

COUNTY COURT.

In presenting the resolutions to the court, EBEN F. RUNYON, ESQ., said:

I hold in my hand the resolutions passed by the members of the *Chicago Bar*, upon the death of the late lamented Colonel Bross. He was your brother and my brother in the profession, and as such we *loved* him. And this is the last act, though sad and solemn, we perform in remembrance of *him*. He was in the prime of life—active, energetic, and ambitious—he strove to place his name upon the scroll of honor—*he has done it*. He died as the hero, statesman or patriot would desire to die—*at his post of duty*.

When I speak of him it is with *sadness*. He was the second man in our beloved profession who extended to me, when a stranger and in a strange city, the baud of friendship—and from that day until his sad death, no unkindly word or thought passed between us. We were ever friends, and in his death we mourn him as a friend and brother. I would to God, I could say of every brother in our profession what I now say of him—*he lived and died an honest sober and Christian man*. But while we mourn his sad and untimely death, we mourn not as those who cannot be comforted. We know that *he still lives—* his bright example is left with us while he marches and countermarches in a world where there is no death.

We mourn his loss—we *weep not over his grave or his remains—* but *because we have them not—*but while we mourn as *friends* and *brothers*, we must recollect that there is one *more dear* than *friend, brother, sister, father* or *mother*, who *mourns*. She mourns a *husband lost, a father to her orphaned child*. The place he so often occupied by her side, is to be *vacant forever*. The child who so often prattled upon his knee, and lisped the dear name of father, will lisp it now in vain—the walls will only echo back the hollow name. Let *us weep* ₁and *mourn with them—*and *our* prayers be *theirs*.

Finally, let me ask that these resolutions, which so tamely represent our love for him who is no more, be spread upon the records of this Court, in remembrance of him who left us but a few days since in the full bloom of health—but who has been so ruthlessly swept from us by rebel hands, j

REMARKS OF JUDGE BRADWELL.

His Honor, Judge BRADWELL, in ordering the resolutions spread upon the records of the Court, said:

The Court, in granting the motion that these resolutions, in relation to the heroic death of Colonel John A. Bross, be placed upon the records of this Court, takes a melancholy pleasure in adding its testimony to the high and richly deserved commendations which have been passed upon him by the resolutions.

He was all and more than the resolutions claim for him—an honored member of the Bar, a true Christian, a noble patriot, and, as a soldier, brave as the bravest.

He went into this contest not because ho loved war, but because ho felt compelled to from a sense of duty. Having counted the cost and knowing the dangers of the situation, he placed himself at the head of a colored regiment, and pledged his life, his all, to the vindication of his country's flag, to the preservation of the Union, and the putting down of the wickedest rebellion that has existed since the day Satan rebelled in Heaven. How well he has kept his pledge, let his noble and heroic death answer.

But while we mourn his loss, we can but rejoice that we live in a country that produces such soldiers, such heroes; that upon the record of his life no blot remains; and that patriots, in all coming time, will bless, revere and honor him.

"He sleeps the sleep that knows no waking," until the trump of the archangel shall call him forth.

In the morning of his days he has sacrificed his life upon the altar of his country's freedom, and now reposes in his last resting-place beneath the fortifications of Petersburgh, which he attempted so bravely to take, but received his death-wound while placing the stars and stripes upon the enemy's works in advance of his regiment. May no flag but the one he loved so dearly and fought so bravely under, ever wave over his remains. If it fever shall, he and all brave men who have died as he did, will have died in vain.

The resolutions of the Bar, and the eloquent remarks of Eben F. Runyon, Esq., will be spread upon the records of the Court as a perpetual memorial of the worth of the late Colonel John A. Bross; and the Clerk Will furnish a copy of them, and of this order, to the wife of the deceased.

CIRCUIT COURT OF COOK COUNTY.

The resolutions adopted at the Bar meeting, and which are given upon a previous page, were presented to the Circuit Coyrt of Cook County, Judge Williams presiding} by H. G. Spafford, Esq., who addressed the court as follows:

May it please the Court:

At a meeting of the Bar of this city, held Upon the death of Colonel John A. Bross, I was appointed to present the resolutions adopted at that meeting to this court, and to ask their enrollment on its records.

Colonel Bross was for many years, and up to the time of his volunteering in the present war, a practitioner in honorable standing at this Bar. His name would not perhaps have been included in an enumeration of a bare few of its most prominent members. He was yet but a young man; there was but little at that time in his bearing or manner of life calculated to attract the public eye. He was a man of modest ways,—who placed no overestimate upon himself,—who year after year went in and out among us, performing in diligence and faithfulness, his duties as a lawyer, as a citizen, as a father and friend,—furnishing no marked indication to others,—perhaps himself unconscious, of the possession of qualities yet destined to give his name a place among the true heroes and martyrs of our history.

From the very beginning of the war, impressed with the magnitude of the approaching conflict, and recognizing among the first, that not by mercenary aid, not by armies gathered from immigrant depots, or the refuse of cities, but only by the devoted efforts of the best and noblest of the land, could the fiery assaults of the South be successfully resisted, he held himself in readiness to

accept any consequences which such opinions, if honestly entertained, would probably, sooner or later, entail upon himself; and when the time came, breaking away at once from all restraints, at the sacrifice of everything but his convictions of duty,—not impulsively, nor borne away by the excitement of the time, nor impelled by ambition, nor even perhaps by the consciousness of any marked personal fitness for such service, but calmly and unostentatiously,—because some must go, and because he could go, he enlisted in the army of the United States.

If the leaders of the rebellion, while they had yet its stormy elements under control, and before their followers had yet been maddened by the taste of blood, could have looked into one such heart, and have had the wisdom soberly to estimate what manner of antagonist it might transform its possessor into in a fitting cause; and could they besides, have recognized that not in scattered instances alone, but over all the North,—in its workshops and offices, in its mines and fields, crowding the streets of its cities, and destined in a few brief days to crowd the ranks of its armies,—there were thousands and tens of thousands actuated by the same purpose,—Who would, when God and their country called, as willingly "crowd the road to death as to a festival," they would not have finally mistaken patience for cowardice, or habits of industry for proofs of degeneracy—they would not have invoked the whirlwind, and then in the midst of it, have pitted the frail shallop of Southern pride and impulse against the integrity, the loyalty and the religion of the North.

Colonel Bross first saw active service while an officer in the 88th regiment of Illinois Volunteers, and as a Captain in that regiment, in the battles of Perryville, Stone River, and Chickamauga, bore himself with distinguished gallantry. Soon afterwards, and while the question whether serviceable troops could be raised from among the blacks was still, with most men, a mooted one, and while something of stigma yet attached, even among ourselves, to those who bore commissions in colored regiments, and while great and peculiar dangers threatened such officers at the hands of the enemy, he asked and obtained permission to recruit the 29th regiment of colored volunteers, becoming himself its Colonel.

I will not more than allude to his faithful efforts, during the months which preceded the first appearance of his regiment upon the field, to bring it up to the proper point of discipline and soldierly knowledge. It is enough to say that he exhibited in the task, the patience and the zeal which might have been expected from one who undertook it conscientiously, and in obedience to opinions long entertained respecting the character and capacity of the colored race. He was unwearied in his efforts to promote the physical comfort and well-being, the self-respect and efficiency of his command;—and nobly did it reward his devotion.

On the 29th of July last, at nine in the evening, Colonel Bross, who was then with his regiment before Petersburgh, received orders to advance and take a position as close as practicable to one of the enemy's forts under which a mine was to be sprung on the following morning. By eleven o'clock the regiment was in its appointed place, sleeping on its arms. It was the first scene in that act of defeat, and of terrible and unavailing slaughter, which forms perhaps, in all its aspects, the saddest passage in this whole war. At five o'clock the next morning, the command having formed behind a belt of woods, moved forward, taking a range of advanced works from the enemy. Sometime afterwards an order came to charge upon a range of fortifications about one hundred yards beyond the line already captured. Timed as it was, it was an ill-advised order.

It was not in the power of that assaulting column successfully to execute it.

It was to the eye of every one there, a desperate undertaking. The word was given,—the bayonets fell to their place,—and

"Into the gates of hell.

Charged the six hundred."

Not many minutes did it take to decide that conflict. They were met by a fire against which no mortal troops could make headway. Corporal Maxwell, carrying the colors, was at once wounded and fell. Corporal Stevens caught them, bore them, to the parapet, and was cut down. Corporal Bailey, who next held them, was instantly either captured or killed. Thomas Barnett, a colored private, seizing them from Bailey, bore them a few steps onward, and fell mortally wounded. Captain Brockway carried them a like distance further, and met the same fate. They then fell into the hands of Colonel Bross. He seized the colors,—waved them above his head, when to touch them was death,—shouted to the quivering troops to rally,— encouraged them with brave words as they gathered round him, and then, the sixth in the succession of those who gave their lives to keep that banner from the dust, himself fell dead. The final repulse ensued. The remnant of our column retreated in rout and utter disorder, the body of Colonel Bross, with those of most of our dead, remaining within the enemy's lines.

The regiment went into the fight four hundred and fifty strong. It lost in the charge, three hundred and twenty, of whom one hundred and fifty- were killed outright. But two of its officers escaped. The loss of the division to which it belonged was forty-one hundred men.

Such, may it please the Court, was the closing scene in the life of one who but yesterday mingled with us in these courts, and whose character was largely the outgrowth of the influences which surrounded him in this community and at this Bar. We were accustomed in years not long past, to read the history of Spartan and Roman achievements,—of those of the days of chivalry,—of Cromwell and his Ironsides, and to institute, with sentiments other than those of unmixed satisfaction, comparisons between them and those of our own day.

In this country especially, we marked the vast increase of wealth, the tendency of men to cities, the extending habits of luxury, the apparent surrender of all hearts and all minds to unheroic occupations and ways of thought, and questioned our ability, should we be called, to meet in the spirit of Hancock, of "Warren and Marion, the requirements of another revolutionary struggle. We little suspected that we were then standing upon the very threshold of a time whose demands would be greater than those of all the past, and that to meet them, there would go forth from around our firesides, from out the circles of our most familiar companionships, from among the men at that moment sitting next to us—walking beside us, those who should be the Hectors and Achilles of a sterner than Trojan conflict,—who should from thenceforth live not in the quiet exercise of home virtues, but amid the carnage, the flash and the thunders of an unequaled war,—who should die in the fore-front of battles, and the memory of whose deeds of transcendent heroism should live in the songs of poets, and be cherished in the hearts of every people until the heavens and the earth should • be rolled together as a scroll.

We could have wished that the living form of our brother could have remained among us until the banner of the Republic had been reinstated upon the ramparts under the shadow of which his body sleeps;—that he who remained firm and trusting through the long night of doubt and disaster, could have been here to behold, with us, this noon of victory. But his eyes have opened upon higher scenes. The Christian patriot has entered upon his reward. It remains for ns, sorrowfully indeed and yet in thankfulness, to ponder the lessons his life and his death are calculated to instill.

I ask the enrollment of the resolutions.

REMARKS OF JUDGE WILLIAMS.

His Honor, JUDGE WILLIAMS, spoke in reply as follows:—

It gives me a melancholy satisfaction to know that by the order I am about to make, there is to be preserved upon the records of this court, in the most enduring form, a tribute to the virtues of our deceased brother, from those who have mingled with him in the intimate relations of professional life.

In this case, the resolutions of the Bar are no mere empty honor, done to a departed comrade. They are the heart-felt and unanimous expression of the love and admiration of those who had been honored by a personal intimacy with the deceased.

For many years I have been well acquainted with our departed friend. Long before his stern sense of duty had impelled him to place himself among that brave army whose warm hearts have been the rampart behind which we have for years securely dwelt, I had learned to prize him highly for the many excellencies which adorned his character. He was possessed of a good mind, and a noble, generous heart. I shall not now speak of him *as the lawyer,* for this has been already appropriately done by others. With capacity sufficient to have enabled him to take a high stand in our profession, he was not content with aspiring merely to professional eminence. It was his ambition to be known to be *a man*—in the broadest sense of that word—a man in character, as well as in intellect. Were I asked— what was the crowning excellence of Colonel Bross? in what did he differ from and excel his competitors? T should reply, *in genuine manhood*. This rendered him as a lawyer, insensible to every motive which would have led him from the path of integrity and honor. This rendered him keenly sensitive to every call of duty. This nerved him for every self- sacrifice. This led him at last cheerfully to offer up his life in the cause of civil liberty.

Of course, in such a manhood, I recognize as the predominant element, Christian principle, ever manifesting itself in loyalty to God, and love to man. That one possessed of such a manhood, should, from the first moment when treason with her bloody fingers clutched at the throat of the Republic, have placed himself unequivocally on the side of the government, was to have been expected. In such a man patriotism would be an ever-welling spring. To such a man loyalty would be significant of something more than a passive obedience to law, and a reluctant, enforced support of the government. It would be synonymous with love. It would mean friendship, fidelity to the Republic; active sympathy with its friends; persistent and determined hostility to its enemies. It is not surprising that such a man should abandon home and friends, should give up professional prospects and personal ease when his country called him to make the sacrifice. It is no matter of wonder that he should endure the privations of the march and the siege; the dangers of the skirmish and the assault; the sufferings of the battle-field and the hospital, without a murmur. All these he accepted as the necessary experience of the soldier. In his own language—"I counted the cost at the beginning; I know its dangers and possible sacrifice; I am one of those who believe that blood must be shed to bring this controversy to a close." And so as Captain in the 88th Illinois he showed himself to be the intrepid soldier in the battles at Perryville and Stone River, and in the bloody fight of Chickamauga. And so in his connection with the 29th United States colored troops, he displayed moral as well as military heroism. And so having deliberately counted the cost, he was [11] ready to be offered up"—a willing sacrifice on his country's altar.

The scene at Petersburgh was but the appropriate ending to such a life. The high sense of duty, the intrepid resolve, the noble self-sacrifice, were manifest even to the last moment.

The foremost man of all his regiment, on the enemy's parapet; bearing aloft with his own hand, the flag that he loved; with the kind cheering words, "*Forward,* my brave boys;" so stood, so spoke John A. Bross in the desperate, hopeless fight at Petersburgh. "*Forward*"—where God called, and duty led; "*forward*"—over heaps of dying and dead; *"forward"*—though his own brave boys were cut down like grain before the siekle; *"forward"*—though five color-bearers in rapid succession had fallen; *"forward"*—against showers of rushing iron and lead; *"forward"*—to probable death, to possible victory. So thought, so acted our deceased friend in the early light of that sad day, when last his form was seen by friendly eyes, his voice heard by friendly ears. So thought, so acted he in civil as well as military life, and so thinking and acting, he was—although he would have been the last to admit it—a Christian *hero*.

Finding it madness to press on with his thinned ranks against the serried lines of the enemy, the same sense of duty which had impelled him forward, now induced him to command a retreat, at the moment that a traitor's ball brought to him instant death, and consigned his body to an unknown, undistinguishable grave. In the highest, truest sense, such a life was an eminent success; such a death, despite all its sad surroundings, was a triumph. He died in an hour of defeat and disaster to his brave followers; in an hour of victory to him. Sadly, the thinned ranks of the 29th fell back at the order for retreat from their loved Colonel; joyfully went upward the emancipated spirit of that Christian soldier at the command "forward" given by One, whom though unseen, he had long loved and obeyed; *"forward"* through the golden gates into his Lord's immediate presence; *"forward"*—to hear the blissful announcement, "Well done, good and faithful servant, thou hast been faithful over a few things, I will make thee ruler over many things: enter thou into the joy of thy Lord."

Ordered, that the clerk enter these resolutions of the Bar upon the record.

LETTER OF DR. MACKAY TO MRS. COL. BROSS.

HEAD-QUARTERS 29TH REGIMENT, U. S. C. V.,

Before Petersburgh, Va., Sept. 22nd, 1864.)

DEAR MRS. BROSS: I am happy to acknowledge the receipt of yours of the 12th inst., and thank you sincerely for the enclosed photograph of my late Colonel.

I have made thorough investigation concerning the letter you conjecture him to have written, and I am led to suppose that it must have been an order.

He *was* "unprecedentedly busy" that week. The whole regiment had been on fatigue often, and had moved camp several times.

I have much pleasure in reflecting upon the many happy hours I spent with him, and will willingly comply with your request, to pen a few of my reminiscences.

The bond of union which existed between us I owe principally to my being a Scot. Among the first things he told me was, that his wife was Scotch, and often he said he hoped to introduce me to his father-in-law, at Sterling.

Once he said: "Doctor, I am glad you're a Scotchman. I said, so was I—wouldn't be anything else for the world. We often took turns reading to each other. Burns generally came to my share, and while I recited or read such pieces as "Death and Doctor Hornbook," "Tam O'Shanter," etc., he, lying on his back, would throw his arms over his head, exclaiming, "o immortal Bobby I who can approach yon?" I got the loan of "Lucille," by "Owen Meredith," and we fairly gloated over it for several days. We were surprised and delighted at the power and beauty of young Bulwer. I had a volume of Scott's "Waverly," "Fortunes of Nigel," and "Peveril of the Peak." He said: "Doctor, it will make the book much more readable, under present contingencies, were it cut in two!" Cut in two it was, and we read them while "marching along" through the "Chickahominy swamps" to the James. I can see him now, as I used to admire him, intent on "Peveril," through the clouds of hot dust. Verily, had his author seen him, he might have taken him for his *"beau ideal"* of some Scotch warrior, with his swarthy, bearded, sunburnt face—the whole figure dust-begrimmed. In his company I never had a weary, flagging hour. He invariably led off with sparkling, cheerful, intellectual conversation. o that this army were officered by such as Colonel Bross! *He* believed that

"Virtue alone ennobles human kind,

And power should on her glorious footsteps wait."

The last time we met was the night before they struck camp for the fight. He rode up to the hospital in company with Major Brown, to whom he introduced me. He looked and felt very happy. He was dressed, for the first time during the campaign, in his full uniform, his valise having just arrived from City Point. I chide him for having performed the anti-patriarchal operation of shaving, having donned the "Burnside cut"—shaving the chin, leaving side whiskers and mustache. I insisted on their staying to supper. It was a very hot afternoon, and I had some iced lemonade, with what we in army *parlance* called, "a brick in it." We sang some hymns and a few Scottish songs lean yet hear his rich bass voice joining in the refrain of "My Nannie's awa." Those few happy moments were too soon spent.

We supped—'twas the last I was to eat with my brave Colonel, and the last table he sat at; for, in his tent, each one sat and ate and lay on mother earth. He said tome, when about to start, "Now, Doctor, we have just got our valises up from City Point, and I *expect a move soon*. Will you have the goodness to take charge of them?" Of course I was happy to do so. He asked me to ride out to camp with him. I did so. 'Twas a happy three miles' ride. The evening was beautiful and cool after the sultry day. We were very lively, and the horses seemed to partake of the spirit of the riders. I said: "Colonel, you'll have a fine staff when it's all full; you must have a pair of eagles at its head." He turned to me, and smiling, said: "Doctor, I'm just going to have them *too. Yes, Sir."* He then congratulated himself upon having his clothes, as he would not feel so bad on going to corps headquarters, as he did with that old blouse." He also remarked: "Doctor, I can sec by the way things are going that you will soon be our brigade surgeon; and then" (laughing) "we'll have more transportation."

The regiment was camped in a pine forest. Captain Aiken and other officers were sitting around the Colonel's tent. I then mentioned that the Medical Director of the corps had desired me to pick out a few good intelligent boys from our division, and give them a few simple lessons in surgery, and I was desirous of having one from our regiment. I asked Captain Aiken for such a one whom I knew to be in his company; but he rather summarily refused. I good-naturedly argued the point with him—it might be for his (the Captain's) own benefit, as well as any one else's, that we should have efficient hospital help. Alas I it turned out so.

But I did not press the matter. The Colonel listened to all, but said nothing. He generally took things coolly. We changed the subject—talked of prospects. Colonel said that there would be an important move before long. It was now getting dark, and preparing to mount, my foot in the stirrup, the Colonel came to my side, and putting his hand on my shoulder, said: "Doctor, don't say anything more about that. I'll give you the boy in a day or two. I see how beneficial it will be to all of us. I thanked him, mounted, we shook hands. "I' 11 send the valises up in the morning, should we move." "All right, Colonel. Come and see us as often as you can at the hospital." "I will; but don't be a stranger, Doctor. Good night—good night." I yet see his tall, manly, broad- shouldered form turn from me in that darkening, dense, Virginian woods.

Ah! truly, what a loss is yours, when one who knew him so short a time learned so to appreciate.

His hospitality and uniform kindness, gentlemanly, straightforward bearing, gained him the high esteem of all. But to me he was more than that. His admiration for everything Scottish, and his grasp of the very soul of Scottish poetry, making often the tear of enthusiasm dance in his eve, was something additional which makes me feel his loss so keenly. How he admired, and *how thoroughly he lived out* the following stanza of Burns:

"Preserve the dignity of man
With soul erect,
And trust the universal plan
Will all direct."

Often we wandered together in those woods, by turns arguing, philosophizing, or reading. Often at the end of a long hot day's march, with our towels, soap and a cup, searching for a bathing-place. Water was very scarce then, and we would pour it from the cup over each other. Then, cooled and refreshed, we would resume our moralizing, etc. Let me tell you a conversation I remember, which struck me as almost prophetic. It took place in company with Adjutant Downing, for whom the Colonel had a very high estimation, and, I think, Captain Aiken, and myself. Our subject was "Death." The Colonel said: 'One thing I wish: if it is my fate to fall before the enemy, I hope I may not have a long, lingering wound. If I'm to die a soldier's death, let me die on the field." Then, laughing, he repeated the last two lines of Campbell's "Lochiel."

Truly do you say, how strictly did he perform his dutj\ With him, everything he did was a duty, and performed well and cheerfully. He has said to me: "How contemptible it is for us to distress ourselves about the littleness and frivolities of life—these things which generally distract the brains of humanity. Our great object should be *ditty energetically and cheerfully performed, unmindful of all consequences.*" "Yes," he said further, "it was an awful sacrifice for me, Doctor, to leave my wife and little one; but it was my duty, and that duty will bo performed."

Intensity was one of his chief characteristics. He loved intensely that which was noble, pure and good; and he was what Carlyle would call a "superb hater" of everything low, vile or mean. Let the rising generation aim at the goal of my late noble Colonel, and farewell all doubt of human progress.

> "He was a hero, and his might
> Tramped on eternal wrong Its way,
> And through the ebon walls of night
> Hewed down a passage unto day."

THE END

Get more great reading from BIG BYTE BOOKS

Made in the USA
Lexington, KY
28 June 2018